Early Praise for

OFF THE BEATEN TRACK

"Off the Beaten Track: My Crazy Year in Asia" is by far Frank's best book yet – a real full on, in your face, vicarious adventure!"

 - Janet Hughes, Amazon reader

"I know you will enjoy the entertaining experiences only Kusy would remain alive to tell."

 - Valerie Caraotta, Top 100 Amazon reviewer

"Another action-packed and funny memoir from Frank Kusy."

 - Amazon reader

"Touches our emotions, sets us off thinking about the true meaning of life."

 - Cherry Gregory, author, *The Girl from Ithaca*

"Fast moving, highly engaging, informative and hysterically funny."

 - Fifi Bergere, Amazon reader

"I know I will read again just because it was so much fun the first time."

 - Quilted Shepherd, Amazon reader

Off the Beaten Track: My Crazy Year in Asia

Frank Kusy

First published in 2014 by

Grinning Bandit Books

http://grinningbandit.webnode.com

ISBN 978-0-9575851-8-8

Cover design by Amygdaladesign

DEDICATION

For my dearest Anna D…with thanks for not pushing me under
that bullet train.

Contents

Map   v

Foreword   vii

The Crazy Polish Biker Chick   1
The King is Down   6
Outward Bound   11
Buddha and the Coca Cola Lady   21
Bali High   27
Java Jive   35
Marco Polo and the Voodoo Bus Driver   42
Big Blag in Kuala Lumpur   52
How to get the Death Penalty in Malaysia   62
Love Shack   66
Stressed out in Samui   75
It's my Job   81
The Unluckiest Man in the World   86
Off the Beaten Trek   94
How to Die in Khao Yai   102
Joss   112
Behind the Veil   115
The Trouble with Trat   121
Big on Frogs   126
The Wackiest Wat   133
Back Home…to Trouble   138
The Neighbours from Hell   143
A New Direction   147
Maria   152
Golf on the Dunes   161
Aliens in India   166
Birth of a Market Trader   178
The Final Curtain   182

A Note from the Author   187
Acknowledgements   189
About the author   190

Map

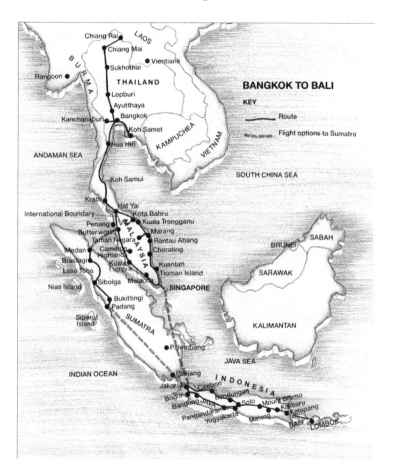

Foreword

I suppose the idea of getting off the beaten track came to me in Penang. Having left my Trailfinders tour group back at the Snake Temple (too many live snakes falling out of the roof for my liking!) I was standing at one of the boat quays, looking out to sea. Just then, a small motorised craft puttered up and about a dozen loud, fat package tourists piled out.

'Hey, mister!' a particularly fat and noisome youth accosted me. 'Where's the nearest Taco Bell?'

I couldn't believe my ears. 'You've come to one of the most beautiful islands in Southeast Asia and all you're interested in is fast food? Don't you want to look around first?'

The boy absent-mindedly scratched a pimple on his face. 'No, we don't. Now, where's the Taco Bell?'

I sighed. 'Penang doesn't have a Taco Bell. But it does have a McDonald's at the top of the new Komtar.'

The group uttered a collective *'Really? That's great!'* And then they all ran off to claim their Double Double Cheese burgers.

Half an hour later, they were back on the boat and zooming off to their next destination, having seen nothing of Penang but a smiley Malay in a perky hat offering them extra Coke and chips if they went 'large'.

'How sad,' I thought to myself. 'Is this what mass tourism is doing to the world? Whatever place I write about, it's going to be overrun with McDonalds, KFCs, coffee shops and 7/11 stores in a few years. My only hope of giving my traveller readers any sense of adventure is to look out venues where no man has gone before.'

There was no doubt about it.

I was going to have to go off the beaten track.

Chapter 1

The Crazy Polish Biker Chick

I didn't really want to write another travel guide. Especially one covering half of SouthEast Asia. But the crazy Polish biker chick was cursing me through the door again. She left me no choice.

It all started innocently enough. Buoyed up with the success of my first book – an oddball diary of my shoestring travel through India with a character called Kevin – and having just completed a travel guidebook on that same country, I sat down one day to write my *magnum opus*. I had no idea what it was going to be about, but it was going to be good. I was going to be a titan amongst writers. I was going to be the next Hemingway or E.M. Forster. I rolled a sheet of crisp new paper into my new portable typewriter, and sat down and waited for the Muse to smite me.

She didn't. I wrote the title, and then my name, and then I thought of a better title and ripped out the page and started again. At this point, my OCD kicked in and I started obsessing about fluffs on the carpet. There was a particularly annoying one at the foot of my Buddhist altar – it had to go. So did the piece of litter just up and to the left of it. It was the corner of an old sweet wrapper: how on earth had I missed that? In the end, I had to hoover the whole carpet. Twice. That was when I knew I had a problem.

*

The crazy Polish biker chick and I hooked up one stormy night when there was a power cut in our house share and we drunkenly collided in the corridor. It was the same night I finally ran out of fluffs to pick off the carpet and had to face up to the grim fact that I was not going to be the next Forster or Steinbeck after all. So I was a prime candidate for an amorous distraction.

Unfortunately, I already had a girlfriend. One who'd been patiently waiting on the sidelines for me to come out of my literary angst and have time for a relationship again. This girl, Anna, was far too good for me – she had got me into Buddhism, along with her sister Brenda, a few years earlier, and had been putting up with all my botched attempts at 'human revolution' ever since. One time, she had almost pushed me under a bullet train in Tokyo – she was that frustrated with my behaviour – and now, when I told her the 'good news' of my new romance, she was going to wish she'd gone ahead and done it.

The Polish biker chick was scary. Long, black hair right down her back, dressed tip to toe in black leather, she made me twang her suspenders and then leapt on me in totally inappropriate social situations. Lifts, bus stands, railway platforms, even bedding stores on Sale Day: everywhere was fair game. Then she would drive me home on her Harley low rider and force-feed me Italian spaghetti to build up my strength again.

All thoughts of writing went out of my head. I was the unwilling love slave of a booted and bodiced Boadicea who would have put a chain round my neck if she could.

There is a term in my Buddhism called *shakubuku*, which loosely means telling other people about the practice, awakening them to their full potential as human beings. 'I've got this girlfriend who *says* she's interested in Buddhism,' I told Dick Causton, the leader of our small Nichiren sect in the UK, 'but all she wants to do when I open up my altar to start chanting to it, is rip my clothes off. What's your take on that?' Dick paused in thought. 'Well,' he chuckled gently. 'There's no rule against…ahem…"horizontal" *shakubuku*, but is it elevating your life-state, or is it elevating something else?'

Still confused, I went to a Buddhist discussion meeting and poured out all my woes to a surprised – and mainly amused – group of virtual strangers. Comments ranged from 'You're complaining?' to 'What's her phone number?' But one young girl, with the most liquid pair of green eyes I had ever seen, took me more seriously. 'There's this quote I found recently by our main man in Japan, Daisaku Ikeda,' she said.

"When we fall in love, life seems filled with drama and excitement. We feel like the leading characters in a novel. But, if you get lost in love just because you are bored, and consequently veer from the path you should be following, then love is nothing more than escapism."

Well, that rang several bells. That was exactly my situation.

'I don't feel like the leading character in a novel,' I found myself sobbing into this girl's arms after everyone else had left. 'I've got into this mess by avoiding having to write one!'

'There, there,' she said, patting me gently on the head. 'Stay here tonight, and take a load off.'

And all of a sudden, staring up into those twin pools of liquid green eyes, I really was lost in love.

*

The biker chick didn't mind about Anna – she seemed to enjoy being the 'other woman', the risky biscuit, the siren who had stolen a man's soul from his first love. But as soon as Nicky came on the scene, she certainly did mind.

'I can hear you in there!' she screamed through the door as Nicky and I began christening my new carpet. 'You say you go in the room to do your chanting! This noise is not chanting. This noise is like sexy noise of buffalo to cow!'

We stopped, and giggled. This was too much fun. What was that crazy biker chick going to say or do next?

The answer was 'plenty'. A pile of steaming hot spaghetti came sliding under my door. Followed by the most eerie and frightening Polish curses through the thin pane of it.

'Pójdź prosto do piekła, skurwysynu! Wygotuję twoje jądra w oleju!' (Go straight to hell, motherfucker. I'm going to boil your testicles in oil!)

And she just would not go away. We could hear her out there, rocking back and forth on her fish-netted knees, moaning and crying like a mad thing.

'Czym sobie na to zasłużyłam? Muszę się zabić, chcę umrzeć!' she shrieked, which roughly translated as 'What have I done to deserve this? I must kill myself, I want to die!'

*

But then she got hungry and forgot about dying. We paused and waited until we heard her thump heavily upstairs to the kitchen, and then I smuggled Nicky out of my ground floor window and out into the street.

'Will you marry me?' I asked her as I lowered her to safety. 'I really think we've got a good thing going.'

'Of course, you idiot,' she laughed back. 'As long as you survive the next twenty-four hours.'

Turning round in my small room, I considered the deep hole I was now in. How was I going to explain myself to Anna, not just about one woman, but two? How was I going to tell the biker chick I had just proposed to someone I'd only just met? And how was I going to tell Nicky that I was so flat-broke, I couldn't even afford a wedding licence?

*

Just then, very fortuitously, the phone rang and saved me from triple trauma.

'We *love* what you've done with India,' enthused my publisher, Paula, down the airwaves. 'How do you feel about doing another one?'

A stone dropped from my heart.

'Yes, please!' I crowed back. 'Where am I going?'

'Bangkok to Bali. How soon can you leave?'

I shivered as the biker chick began howling at my door again.

'How about right now?'

Chapter 2

The King is Down

Zoom, zoom, zoom, I was zipping down the road on a maniac motorbike, whizzing in and out of the traffic, dodging mile upon mile of stranded cars and taxis in downtown Bangkok. It was the rush hour and I knew it was a risk, but these nippy two-wheelers were the only way through. The driver was on speed, he *had* to be, and I hadn't got a helmet. We came to a set of lights, and it was yellow, no, it was *red*, and he was going too fast to stop—just ploughed on through and skidded into this long white stretch limo with diplomatic flags on top. I just had time to register a small frightened figure in the back of the limo, wearing a high plumed hat with a feather on it, and then crash, bang, wallop—we went straight into the side of him. I fell off the back of the bike, skidding my tailbone on the tarmac, and the driver, well, he was pinned to the bonnet and a whole load of guns were pointed at his head. 'How exciting!' I thought. 'It's like that film *Alien*, but instead of all those guns pointing at a giant monster from a different galaxy, they're pointing at a tiny little Thai guy with bad teeth and a fag hanging out of his mouth. But hang on, why are they starting to point some of those guns at me?'

Nobody venerates their king like the Thais. I'd even heard

6

of them attacking a foreign tourist who dropped a ten baht coin and who stamped on it to stop it rolling away. Unfortunately, for the tourist, he'd stamped on the side of the coin with the king's head on it, and they beat him half to death on the pavement.

With horror, it dawned upon me that King Bhumipol himself was in that limo, and that the security guards advancing on me were not smiling. This was not good.

'Terrorist attack on our beloved king!' I sat in their van, imagining the next day's headlines. 'Motorbike taxi makes daring attack on our beloved sovereign! Foreign tourist held for questioning! In an unprecedented raid, two villainous assassins—posing as a motorbike driver and his foreign passenger—have just charged a convoy of vehicles bound for the airport and tried to kill the king! His royal highness was rushed to safety after the cowardly assault, and is reported to be in "stable condition". The bike rider faces the customary death penalty, and his tourist accomplice the maximum jail sentence allowable by law. The tourist has been named as Mr Francis Kusy of Surrey, England, and his only comment to date has been: "What a buzz! Best ten minutes of my life!"'

I also imagined a voicemail message from my mother in England:

'Dear Son, It was very rude of you to put the phone down on me. It's no good saying "Help! They won't let me speak anymore and are putting me in chains!" I know the real reason—you have time for everybody else, but not your own mother. All I got from you was that you were sitting in a police cell in handcuffs, and you didn't know why. Haven't you heard the news? It's all over the TV! I don't know what you were thinking, but it was quite irresponsible of you hitting that poor king. He didn't deserve it, and we didn't bring you up that way. Your father and I are very disappointed in you, and you won't be getting that new car we promised you for Christmas. You are obviously not safe behind a wheel. I am especially concerned that you weren't wearing a helmet—you could have had an accident. Some nice man from the British Embassy just phoned to say that you will be detained, quote, "indefinitely". Does that mean you'll miss my birthday? The neighbours are already talking and I don't know what to tell them. For God's sake, when *will* you grow up?'

I directly inherited the travel bug from my mother. She it was who, following the death of my Polish father, took me on a long series of holidays all around Europe – a different country every summer – until, quite suddenly, she re-married a totally unadventurous man and had her wings clipped for the next 25 years. I guess she was a bit jealous of this because she totally disapproved of my later travels – especially my first trip to India four years earlier, when I'd had my head shaved for a laugh and sent her a photo of my billiard-ball bonce.

'I am afraid I do not share the "joke"', she wrote huffily. 'As a matter of fact, I had a good cry. If you're getting catcalls even in India, imagine the response back here in England. You look like a convict, or a skinhead. It takes at least six months to grow a little hair, and meanwhile you're supposed to be looking for a job. Who will employ you looking like this? Incidentally, it was Mother's Day on Sunday. This makes three years in succession that you have forgotten.'

My dear old mum. I thought of her fondly as the security guards emptied my wallet, found my Press card, and decided to let me go. She would have loved all this.

But no, on reflection, she wouldn't. Only that morning, I had received a very disappointed communication:

'Anna phoned me today. She was upset, and told me about

your letter, breaking up the relationship. I could only sympathise with her, and suggest she wait and see what happens when you return. You can imagine my surprise when I received your last letter, telling me that you have now proposed marriage to someone else – who is Nicky? – and that you have shaved your head again. What is Asia doing to you? I am most puzzled. How can you break up a long and intimate relationship one day, and on the next, ask a different girl to commit herself for life? Full marks for nerve, son. What have you to offer this new girl on your return? No job, no home, no money, no prospects – and no hair. I am sorry to write like this, but it seems such irresponsible behaviour. At the moment, you are far way in a different world, and probably very lonely. So postpone any other impulsive decisions until you return, please. And please try and grow some hair before you come back!'

*

Yes, I had shaved my head again. But this time it was a complete accident.

I had spotted the hair dye whilst wandering around Foodland supermarket in Sukhumvit at midnight. It was a Japanese brand called Bigen, and it cost only 60 pence for five applications. The first one stained the entire sink a dark brown, and half the toilet too. The second one worked okay, but it left the whole bathroom looking like an abattoir. Even my pillow was stained black in the morning.

It was during the second application – while I was standing by the sink, stark-naked and with blood-coloured dye running down my head and torso – that I heard the knock at the door. It was a timorous knock, suggestive of someone who didn't really want to come in. I didn't stop to think, just grabbed a small hand-towel and ran off with it, coyly clutching it to my loins. As the door opened, I was confronted by a tiny room-maid holding two trays of food meant for someone else. I looked at her, she looked at me, and then she dropped the trays with a shriek, and ran off down the corridor, pressing every alarm button in sight. Moments later, just as I was cleaning myself off, there was another knock at my door, this time a much more insistent one. 'Where is BODY?' demanded the burly security guard as I opened up. 'Where you hide BODY?' Three other guards then piled in and began turning my room over – peering into cupboards, looking under the bed, even leaning out the windows. It took me quite some time – with the hotel being evacuated, police sirens kicking off in the street below, and fellow guests shouting 'Murderer!' at me from down the hall – before I finally convinced them that I hadn't killed any-body.

I had simply dyed my beard.

But that wasn't the end of the story. That sudden knock at the door had caused my razor to slip as I was trimming my temples, and a big ridge of bare flesh had opened up above my left ear. 'Oh dear,' I thought. 'That doesn't look good. I better even that up with a bare right temple.' And before I knew it, I had evened up my whole head and left it quite bald. Which turned out to be a good thing, because when all those fellow guests looked around for the murdering idiot who'd ruined their sleep over breakfast, they didn't recognise me at all.

Chapter 3

Outward Bound

Ian, the leader of the tour group I joined in Bangkok, didn't like my shiny dome. 'Is that because you're a Buddhist?' he said distrustfully. My reply – 'No, it's because I couldn't think of anything better to do at two o clock in the morning.' – didn't seem to satisfy him.

The other thing that didn't seem to satisfy him was that I was an 'observer'; I wasn't officially part of his group. Paula, my publisher, had cut a deal with an up-and-coming travel agency in London, Trailfinders, and I was to both write her a book and plug the 15-day 'Router' tour that Trailfinders were trying out between Bangkok and Bali.

Ian was particularly concerned at the small Walkman I kept shoving up his nose. 'Don't quote me on that,' became his familiar litany at the end of each discourse he gave the group, and he made me swear on my Buddhist bible not to put his name in the book.

Not that his discourses were lewd or unsavoury or politically incorrect or anything. He just knew that some subjects – notably prostitution in Thailand – were very sensitive and 'bound to be misinterpreted.'

'So you're a Buddhist?' he taunted me our first night. 'Do

you meditate on your navel, then, and where's your begging bowl?'

'I'm not that kind of Buddhist,' I said stiffly. 'I chant to improve myself and for world peace.'

'World peace?' scoffed the tall, squinty-eyed naysayer. 'That's an infinite amount of bullshit. I mean, there's an average of about 46 wars going on around the world at any one time. How are you going to stop that?'

What I should have said – and hindsight is a wonderful thing – was 'Buddhism is reason. Well, our form of Buddhism is, anyway. We recognise that a third of the planet will always be addicted to the three poisons of greed, anger and stupidity. But it is our hope, that if one by one people do their "human revolution" and change themselves for the better, there will come a day when the other two-thirds of the planet are either Buddhists or supportive of Buddhists. Then the cycle of war will be broken forever.'

What I actually said was, 'Well, I'm doing my best, innit?'

Which really got Ian on my case. In fact, he wasn't happy until he had trapped me into denouncing Zen (a type of Buddhism I had no knowledge of, or interest, in) as intellectual, narrow and without meaning.

'Call yourself a Buddhist?' he said with a wicked grin. 'How can you be so *judgemental?'*

*

The next morning, I met the rest of the Trailfinders group, and what an interesting collection of people they were. First, there was an elderly American called Paul who looked exactly like Cecil B. De Mille. 'Uh,' he said as he reached the hotel. 'Wut's the *mechanics* of checkin' in?' Paul was accompanied by his smiley, balding son Andy, who seemed to be some kind of CIA operative. 'My business is artificial intelligence,' he told us secretively. 'But I don't want that in my passport.' We asked him why not, and he said 'I don't wanna be stuck on a plane somewhere and hijacked with the word *"intelligence"* in my passport.'

The rest of the group were all British – two nurses (Alison and Janet), one doctor (Tracy), one teacher recently returned from India (Bridget), and a mild-mannered English accountant called Hugo, with whom I would be sharing digs.

I liked Hugo. A tall, awkward figure with horn-rimmed spectacles and a slouching, gangling gait, he had never travelled outside London before and was naiveté personified. 'Is is okay to drink the tap water here?' he asked innocently, and I said, 'Yes, if you want to die. Did you check the colour of the river on the boat over to our hotel? It gives brown a whole new meaning!'

We were back on the Chao Phaya river for much of the first day – running up from the elegant Oriental Hotel to the rather less elegant Thonburi Snake Farm in a smelly petrol boat which puttered in and out of the narrow *klongs* (waterways) like a slow, meandering bee. I diligently took notes as we did the standard tour of Bangkok – the touristy Floating Market, the even more touristy King's Palace and Temple of the Golden Buddha – but my heart wasn't in it. 'This stuff's been done to death by all the other guidebooks,' I thought, suppressing an inner yawn. 'When are we going somewhere not crawling with tourists?' Even taking up a dare to have a large cobra draped over me at the Snake Farm failed to move me. Its fangs had been removed and it was no danger to anybody.

My interest began to pique a little when we caught the 6.30pm train from Bangkok's Hualamphong station up to

Chiang Mai, 700 kms to the north. 'This is more like it!' I silently rejoiced. 'I'm going to meet some hill tribes!' But Ian did not share my enthusiasm. He was sitting with a German traveller he couldn't stand. So he came over talk to the rest of us and to give Hugo a small, green chilli pepper. 'There's no entertainment on the train,' he said. 'So we'll watch Hugo sweat over his chilli for 15 minutes.'

Poor Hugo. He hadn't the sense to refuse Ian's kind gift, and he had no idea that our malevolent leader had hand-picked a particularly strong *phrik kii noo* chilli pepper. Downing it in one, we all watched in horror as the pale, white accountant's face went a bright beetroot red, and his knees started jigging up and down under the table.

'Don't do that,' Ian chided him. 'We won't be able to play Scrabble.'

Scrabble? Was he serious?

Well, yes he was, and before too long there were seven people playing at once, excited shrieks of 'You don't spell algorithm with a "y"!' and 'There's no such word as kumquat!' filling the air. At one point, I found myself simultaneously eating supper, deflecting Ian's racist jokes, listening to Alison's advice on how to win at Scrabble, comparing notes on Indian *thali* meals with Bridget, taping information for my guidebook, talking to Hugo about Buddhism, and getting sozzled on a huge bottle of Mekong whisky...before adding a 'q' to the word 'at' to clinch final victory.

'What's a *qat?*' said Ian, a look of profound doubt on his face.

'It's a flowering plant native to East Africa and the Arabian peninsula,' I replied, mentally thanking my mother for this trivial piece of information. 'I thought everybody knew that.'

*

As we drew into Chiang Mai the next morning, Hugo woke me with a well-aimed pillow to the head. My alarm had gone off, but my earplugs had stopped me hearing it. Then he put aside a yellow-lined sleeping bag, a pair of vermilion socks, and a pair of trucking boots – the items he'd decided to 'donate' to the needy hill tribes we'd soon be meeting.

Looking out the train windows, the scenery was spectacular – a ghostly vista of misty mountains, glistening paddy fields, and motionless water buffalo, broken only by the occasional palm tree or raised house on stilts. 'Yes, this is definitely more like it,' I grinned to myself. 'Not a tourist in sight.'

But then we got into Chiang Mai proper and it was simply heaving with foreign travellers. I was shocked. Disco bars, ping-pong palaces, all-night parties – it was like a mini-Bangkok! 'What's going on *here?*' I asked Ian, and he said, 'It's been like this since the 60s, when the Americans turned Chiang Mai into an R & R base from Vietnam. Put up with it, it's the last taste of civilisation you'll have for the next few days.'

Last taste of civilisation? That cheered me up. I even did an impromptu *Ramwong* circle dance on the stage of the Old Chiang Mai Cultural Centre, I was that happy.

The following morning, we drove out to Mae Yai waterfall – 200 feet of beautiful cascades and rushing water – where we began our big trek. 'Will there be spiders?' asked Hugo nervously, and Ian comforted him by saying, 'No, but lots of snakes.' Indeed, as we plunged into the lush, vivid-green jungle, our guide Pang – who was going ahead – could be seen flicking lethal green snakes off the rocky path with his stick: first impaling them and then hanging them to die on branches.

'It's like the final scene of *Spartacus,*' I commented to Bridget. 'I wonder if Pang was Crassus in a former life?'

Every so often, the dense forest tree-line broke to reveal a cluster of wooden village huts, out of which swarmed hosts of shy, giggling children with Mongolian features. They were of the White Karen tribe, and they were deliriously happy to see us.

They weren't happy for very long. Later on, after we'd washed off in a nearby stream and moved into the large hut on stilts provided for us, those children wanted to sing us some songs. Then they wanted us to sing them some songs back. All went well until it came to my turn. I should be able to sing, I was born on the same day as Dean Martin and Barry Manilow. But no, I can't, and when I stood on the table and broke into my rendition of 'Old McDonald had a Farm', the faces of those dear little village children began to crease and crumple and their eyes filled with tears. 'Here a piggy, there a piggy, everywhere a piggy, piggy,' I croaked with gusto, and then I did my 'Oink, Oink' piggy noises and half my frightened audience ran off screaming.

'Here come taxi!' said the headman the next morning, announcing the arrival of our elephants. Huge, hulking beasts, they were, with independent, strong-willed natures. My elephant was called 'Flash', which was a complete misnomer. Flash never moved faster than an exhausted snail. Hugo's elephant, by contrast, alternated between spraying him with river water (it was a very hot elephant) and running off into the jungle looking for tender shoots to eat. Hugo eventually managed to control his beast by gripping his red socks and jamming his jackboots into its head. It looked very uncomfortable. As for Tracy, well, all we heard from her were regular bleats of alarm which rose to an orgasmic ululation as she forgot which ear to jiggle the elephant under (to get it moving) and sent it stampeding off at a gallop. About the only person happy with their pachyderm was Bridget – 'What scenewy!' she lisped. 'Twuly wesplendent! And it was true, because on top of our elephants we could see above the foliage and take in the beautiful valley beyond – a picturesque combination of woodlands, mountains and exotic greenery. Colourful clusters of butterflies floated up to us, and the air was alive with the sound of bees, hornets, dragonflies and cicadas.

At the next village, Pang set up an opium session for Hugo, Bridget and me. A furrow of concern etched itself into Hugo's forehead. 'Opium?' he said. 'Do you think I'll need to take my contact lenses out?'

We wandered up to the headman's hut and found a man lying in a foetal position, packing the resinous poppy pods into a thin clay pipe. Hugo was the first to try it. 'For once, he doesn't look like an English commuter,' said Bridget, a wry smile on her face. 'I'm in training,' retorted Hugo. 'All the top accountants in the UK are into this stuff!'

17

Later, mildly intoxicated, I found myself on the head of the lead elephant, called Speedy Gonzales, who raced ahead, had an enormous crap on the path, and then wandered off to munch bamboo in a shady glade while everybody else caught up.

But not everybody else was catching up. Andy was spread-eagled over his elephant in an attitude of crucifixion, and Janet had been plucked off her beast by a branch and was hanging out of a tree. The only person who eventually drifted up the join me was Hugo, who had got back on his elephant and who was wearing a milky-eyed look of contentment.

He'd had the extra pipe.

*

I was beside myself with happiness. 'What an adventure!' I privately exulted. 'Just about anything could happen out here. I can't wait to write this up and share it with my readers!'

But my happiness was short-lived. The next village we came to, we found a party of package tourists already there – all clicking away with Nikons and peering into private family huts.

'What happened to your "last taste of civilisation"?' I tackled Ian with more than a degree of annoyance. 'It's like a bloody convention!'

It was the first time I saw the stoic tour leader's cool slip.

'I was afraid of this,' he confided darkly. 'There are over 100 trekking agencies in Chiang Mai, and as soon as we open up a new trail they come along and find us. It's getting to be a real problem.'

Problem? Well, yes, it certainly was a problem. How was I going to recommend an area which was rapidly being taken over by swarms of tourists? I didn't know how I was going to do it, but one day, I determined, I would be coming back here to blaze a trail of my own…

*

By the time we got to Tha Ton, close to the Burmese border, we were like Agatha Christie's *Ten Little Indians.* Old Paul had gone home with a bad cold, Anne was limping from a sprained ankle after falling down a ditch, Bridget was having a fit of anxiety after losing her purse in a Buddhist monastery (of all places) and Hugo, Alison and Tracy had been struck down with diarrhoea. I mentally congratulated myself on only drinking Mekong whisky the previous night – the village water had looked decidedly dicey.

By nightfall, only Andy, Ian and I were left unscathed. And that didn't last long either, because as soon as we checked into *Thip's Travellers House,* Ian got mauled by Mrs Thip's 'pet' mountain cat after trying to make friends with it. 'Who's next?' I joked to Andy, and he said, 'Probably me. Have you seen the size of those mosquitoes? Pass some of that repellent over, I'm gonna goop up my legs before they eat me alive!'

Mrs Thip was a force of nature – a small, squat, wide-grinned woman with more drive and ambition than Napoleon. She'd tried farming, like 80 per cent of Thais, but it hadn't paid. So she'd begun setting up river-rafting trips down the Kok River and then setting up a guest house here in Tha Ton. It was Mrs Thip's goal in life to take over the whole of north Thailand. 'I go far,' she told me. 'First I get video, then sky is limit! I am business woman, I look far. I am good Buddhist, so not allowed to kill. But I am allowed to kill other guest houses with business!'

Mrs Thip may have been an old pirate, but she was red-hot

on information. 'River fed by mountain water,' she informed us. 'Good for swimming – no crocodiles!' While we were thinking about that one, she said we must visit the Morning Market, which was the place to buy 'mountain food' like wild pig, snake and iguana. 'You can have dead,' she chirped cheerfully, 'or you can take home and kill yourself!'

I couldn't quite work out why Ian had taken us to Tha Ton. Okay, it was a scenic little spot, surrounded by dense jungle and rolling hills, but he wouldn't let us go river-rafting – 'The water's too choppy, half the rafts don't come back' – and he wouldn't let us watch any of Mrs Thip's blood-curdling Chinese videos, to which she was addicted. Instead, he made Andy and me climb back up the steep staircase to the Buddhist monastery to recover Bridget's purse. Fortunately, we found it. Unfortunately, a big party kicked off up there – local youths playing strange jungle music on modern drum-kits – which went on till midnight. Then, at 4am, an immense gong woke up the monks and everyone sleeping within a one kilometre radius.

Chapter 4

Buddha and the Coca Cola Lady

It was back in Bangkok that I discovered that I was on the wrong tour.

'What do you mean I'm on the wrong tour?' I asked Ian.

'It's news to me too,' he said, scratching his bald head. 'Trailfinders are running two experimental tours – one to North Thailand and one from Bangkok to Bali. The latter one doesn't start for another three days. I guess they thought you – and they – could benefit from giving you a taster of both!'

Well, I wasn't too upset, I'd enjoyed a bit of rough in the North. And as it turned out, it was the *only* bit of rough I was to experience over the next 15 days.

Unless, of course, one counted Ian's 'leaving party' down in Patpong, Bangkok's famous red-light area.

This was an experience none of us would forget in a hurry. The first club we visited, tellingly called 'Pussy Galore', had all the girls squirming in embarrassment and Hugo staring into his beer glass, where a ping pong ball had just landed. The deliverer of the ping pong ball, a happily smiling go-go dancer with her legs wide open, was most pleased with her aim and indicated that she could do it again.

'Well, this is interesting,' I told myself. 'I guess I ought to start doing some research for my book.' But I was not looking forward to it. My own experience of strip clubs was limited to a single visit in Soho, London, when I had dragged my brother John in for a laugh and had left in complete embarrassment. The stripper had spotted our adolescent shyness and had begun imitating it, much to the amusement of the other punters.

I settled, on Ian's recommendation, on a club called Cleopatra. This had nine bare girls with flower-garlanded hair, jiving mechanically to disco music on a narrow strobe-lit stage. The audience were mostly balding, middle age men, and more than a few of them had a girl or two jigging up and down in their lap.

Cleopatra was run by a happy, twinkle-eyed, rascally 'Mama San' called Jean, who spoke surprisingly good English.

'Call me Gin,' she quipped with a wink. 'Like the drink we do not have.'

'What you do have,' I said, looking around the packed club, 'is all sorts of *farangs* (foreigners). 'Which nationality do you like best?'

Jean gave a sniff. 'No like English – too stingy. No like Americans – noisy, big mouth, and get angry easy. I like German and Australian men best – they spend most money.'

Jean's eyes flitted to and fro while I interviewed her. She was watching over her girls like a broody hen. I expected her to clam up when I asked the touchy subject of how much she considered a fair price for their services, but no, she was quite candid. 'One thousand baht (£20), not one baht less. My girls are good, clean girls, not from gutter!' And where did her girls take their customers? Jean confided that most of them ended up in the car park of the nearby Star Hotel. She also confided that her 'lovemaking' show – involving a hunky stud and lissom lady in full sexual intercourse on stage – embarrassed most of her customers. 'It make them think what they are all doing here…and of what they all wish to be doing themselves!'

I personally found Jean's show pretty tasteful. Well, as tasteful as Patpong could get. And one really had to admire the courage of those girls. It took real guts to stand on a lit stage stark naked except for a Chinese riverboat hat and a light silk wrap, with nothing else to do but gyrate round a pole and playfully tweak other girls' nipples. Down on the floor, the hostesses who were distributing Coca Cola and whisky (at horribly inflated prices) were amusing themselves by tying bits of cloth and string into one tourist's hair, while a party of fat Germans dressed up as stallions, and reared and snorted their way into the toilet, never to reappear.

At 10.30pm, Cleopatra's special '3 in 1' show came on. This comprised: a) a girl with a lit Christmas sparkler twinkling between her spread-eagled legs, while Perry Como sang 'Happy Birthday to You'; b) three lesbians soaping each other in a large tub; c) an athletic couple making it energetically in the corner.

At this point, having run out of questions to ask Jean, I made to leave. But no such luck. Two chunky, naked ladies came out of nowhere and straddled both my knees, pinning me to my seat.

'Where did you come from?' I gurgled helplessly.

'You handsome boy,' purred one of them. 'Buy lady Coca Cola?'

I thought on my feet, even though I wasn't standing on them.

'Sorry, no,' I said. 'Me Buddhist.'

It was lucky that my head was still bald, and that I looked the part.

'Oh, you *Buddha!*' cried both girls, leaping off my lap. 'You no *like* Coca Cola lady!'

I interviewed several more clubs over the following nights, but with diminishing interest (they were all pretty much the same) and with an increasingly bad taste in my mouth. It was not that I was prudish, but my mother had raised me to have a decent respect for women, not to watch them prance around naked on stages or imagine them committing unspeakable acts of carnality in car parks. What on earth was the attraction, I found myself thinking. Why were so many men driven to come to this part of the world to indulge in such sordid activity?

Before too long, I would be finding out for myself.

*

The second Trailfinders tour was fun, if a bit rushed. Over half the 15 days were spent in planes, trains and buses, and over half the other half lounging in pools or getting pissed in discos, but I didn't mind. I'd be coming back this way on my own later on – I could do all my guidebook research then. We didn't see much of Thailand – just a quick view of the seaside port of Hua Hin – and even less of Malaysia, but then we crossed from Singapore to Jakarta and suddenly the tour slowed down and became a lot more interesting.

For one thing, our alcoholic new leader, Steve, absconded with one of our number, a pretty young Brazilian girl called Edie. We didn't know where or when they had gone – it was like the *X Files,* they just plain vanished, possibly abducted by aliens and taken away to repopulate a different planet.

In their absence, with no-one else experienced enough to handle complicated travel itineraries, I took charge. I phoned

Trailfinders in London, got everyone's forward travel confirmed (and their hotel bookings) and settled back for what I thought would be an easy ride.

How wrong I was. First, John, the young Scottish guy who went everywhere in red, blue and white Union Jack boxer shorts, had his passport stolen in Jakarta. 'I was standing in this bus,' he recounted, 'when three youths got on, pulled out very sharp knives, and wandered up and down the aisle relieving passengers of watches, jewellery and in my case, passport. I thought I was going to die!'

Then, when we got to Mount Bromo (a day late, because of having to get John a temporary passport), I managed to lose someone else down a volcano. It was all my fault – I really shouldn't have downed a malaria tablet on an empty stomach at four in the morning. It made me feel so ill, I let the rest of the group go ahead and since nobody anticipated a thin two foot rim at the top of the crater and no safety barrier, the first person up – a sunny young girl called Sally – just walked into the volcano…and down it. Suddenly, Sally wasn't sunny anymore and her screams of anguish echoed round the huge black hole as she clung to a ledge by her fingernails. 'Oh dear,' I thought as we flung down a rope and gently helped her back up. 'I really should have given her the torch.'

But the thing that really bothered me about being an (impromptu) tour leader was that I couldn't have fun anymore. No more pools and bars and discos for me – I had to make sure everyone got to bed at a sensible time and got up for the next bus or sightseeing trip in the morning. The only thing that was holding me together was the knowledge that Nicky, my darling Nicky, would be on a plane to Bali in a few days.

I could hardly wait.

Chapter 5

Bali High

Nicky had taken it well, I must say. It wasn't often that a girl got a wedding proposal one day, and the next, her hubby-to-be was on a plane to the other side of the world for three months.

'You go ahead, darling,' she'd said when I broke the news of our enforced parting. 'I've got a bit of money saved up. What say I fly down to meet you in Bali? We can have a pre-wedding honeymoon!'

I'd nodded in happy agreement. 'That would be great! And look, I just got this advance royalty cheque of two-and-a-half grand. Now we can afford to get married in style!'

But waiting for Nicky in Bali was torture. Having crossed through the rest of Java without further incident, and with a shamefaced Steve having returned (minus Edie) to close down the tour, I suddenly felt at a loss. It was hard to explain, but as Steve got all 16 of us together for a farewell meal at Kuta Beach, and the emotional security of the group began to disintegrate, an overpowering mood of sadness swept over me. 'This is no fun,' I thought glumly. 'No news from Nicky, no idea if she's still coming or not, and nobody to keep me company while I kick my heels and wait.'

But then Scottish John, and two of the Trailfinders girls,

Jackie and Anne, said they were hiring a jeep to tour the island, and would I like to come?

Well, yes I would. It was exactly the distraction I needed. First, however, I had to report on Kuta, the tourist centre of Bali. And it was not an easy report to make. It was bad enough walking through the Benidorm style town of frenetic bars, noisy discos, and beer-swilling Australians holding frog-leaping competitions in the high street, but then I came to Kuta Beach itself, and here it was that I gauged the full horrors of tourism. The rudenesses of drunken surfers had rubbed off on the locals and it was impossible to sit on the sand for more than five minutes without being hassled to buy something or insulted if you didn't.

Then I looked around and reconsidered. If – like a lot of travellers seemed to be doing – you let the locust swarm of traders, massage ladies and hawkers wash over you without protest, you could have your hair plaited and beads, your fingers and toes manicured, your whole body massaged with sun-oil, you could buy your gaily-coloured sarong, beach shorts, swimsuit and souvenirs, you could drink your cold beer, have a newspaper delivered, buy a big bag to get all your gear back to the hotel – you could do all this for less than £10 and from the comfort of your newly purchased 180 x 60cm beach-mat!

*

'You can't go off the beaten track in Bali,' Steve had told me. 'The whole island is cultivated to grow crops. There's nothing "wild" about it anymore.'

What he didn't tell me, and this came as a very pleasant surprise, was that 5kms out of Kuta, John and the girls and me were suddenly in the rice fields. Everyone was laughing and smiling and shouting 'Hello, mister! How are you?' Mile upon mile of glistening green rice paddies unfurled before us, along with immaculately laid-out plantations of rubber, bananas, coconuts and cloves. 'Wow, this is the real Bali!' John enthused as he drove the jeep through this magical landscape, and we all grinned in happy agreement.

Passing the craft villages of Celuk and Mas, we came to Ubud, the cultural centre of Bali, and saw the famous *Kecak* or monkey-dance. One hundred men seated in a dark, torch-lit circle, chanting, clapping, hissing and shouting in perfect poly-rhythmic harmony. It was quite a spectacle!

Over the following few days, we pretty much covered all of the island – from the bat cave at Goa Lawah (where thousands of the creatures were in a flap or hanging out), to the wonderfully clean and golden-sand beach of Candi Dasa with (as yet) not a single annoying hawker or massage lady on it, and finally to the black volcanic sands of Lovina Beach right at the top of the island.

'Why are we the only people in the water?' observed Anne, as we stripped off for a nice, cool dip. 'Look, none of the locals are going in!'

I chuckled. 'Oh, Steve told me about that. The Balinese are superstitious, spirit-fearing animists, apparently. Not many of them will go swimming because there are too many mind-boggling monsters in the sea!'

As soon as we got back down south to Denpasar, Bali's smelly capital, I checked in at the GPO for news from Nicky. There was none. Instead, I got two other letters – an angry one from Anna and an even angrier one from my mother, who wanted to know why I was still 'gallivanting round Asia' when I 'should be back home getting a proper job.'

Oh, my supportive mother. She should have known the answer to that one. I was doing what I always did when under pressure from women – fleeing to foreign climes. And she it was who had set the trend. Fifteen years earlier, I had tried running away from her loving but very smothering presence to a Welsh university. Not far enough, as it happened, since she followed me up there every weekend, fighting her way through a scrum of rugby fans at Cardiff station to replace my laundry. Then, a year or so later, I ran away to an Israeli kibbutz to escape my first girlfriend, Addy, who wanted marriage and kids when I wanted the exact opposite.

But it wasn't only women I was running away from. It was pretty much everything my mother represented. Yes, the smaller part of me did want a safe, happy job and a settled, mature relationship, but the greater part of me hated feeling trapped in any one set of circumstances – professional or romantic – and craved total freedom. I was beginning to really enjoy my new unfettered existence where every day brought new adventures, new challenges. The only thing that concerned me, that broke my mood of 'Hey, I'm freewheeling Frankie, I'm having a ball!' was Nicky. I was missing that girl so badly, but hadn't heard from her since I'd left the U.K. over a month ago. Where the hell was she?

At the height of my insecurity, the night before Nicky was supposed to arrive – and still having received no letter – I took the cheap engagement ring she'd given me off my finger. And was immediately accosted by a very pretty Balinese girl in a disco. 'You nice boy!' she said, tugging at my shoulder. 'You come home with me!'

I immediately put the ring back on my finger.

*

The following day, I stood nervously at Ngurah Rai airport. 'What if she's not coming?' I angsted. 'What if she's found someone else? What if she didn't have the heart to tell me?'

But I needn't have worried. There, rushing towards me through the crowd of new arrivals, was a familiar pint-sized figure with a quirky grin – Nicky!

'OhGodOhGodOhGod,' she shrieked as she threw herself into my arms. 'I'm here! It's really happening!'

'I can't believe it myself!' I cried, holding her smiling face in both hands and smothering it with kisses. 'But why didn't you write? I thought something horrible must have happened!'

'I *did* write. I wrote you half a dozen letters!'

'That's strange,' I croaked through my emotion. 'I didn't get them. Who did you address them to?'

'Frank Cosy,' she said. 'That's right, isn't it?'

No sooner had Nicky got off one plane, than she was on another one – a short 20-minute hop to the neighbouring island of Lombok, famous as a jump-off point to see Komodo dragons. We didn't see any Komodo dragons. All we saw for three days was the inside of a luxury bungalow on the paradisical Sengiggi Beach.

'Ooh, this is nice,' said Nicky, as we sat in the sunken bath and threw bubbles at each other after yet another round of steamy sex. 'I could live here forever!'

'It certainly beats Bexleyheath,' I agreed. 'Here, pass that bar of soap. I've just thought of a new use for it…'

*

I didn't know about getting married in style, but Nicky and I got married anyway – and in the strangest of circumstances. As we made our way back to Bali, and up to the cooler environs of Ubud, I had no idea how strange it was going to be.

Igeda, the manic little manager of our lodge in Ubud, went all aquiver when he found out that Nicky was a musician. Not just any musician, mind you, but a contrabassoon player in the Young Musicians Symphony Orchestra. 'Oh, you must learn play gamelan!' he cried, clapping his hands together with joy. 'It is bestest music of the world!'

Well, that idea went down a storm with Nicky. The gamelan bands of Bali were famous – she couldn't wait to be one of those turbaned, cross-legged, and colourfully sashed musicians gonging away on tinny xylophones.

There was however one problem.

'Number one gamelan band is in village of Menyali, two hour drive north of here,' Igeda told us. 'But this one no possible…so sorry.'

'Why no possible?' Nicky was crestfallen.

Igeda gave an apologetic sigh. 'Menyali band play for only three thing. Birth, death, and marriage.'

Nicky looked at me, and I looked at her, and in one breath we said: 'We're getting married!'

I have never been an impulsive person – indeed, my passport should have had 'Mister Cautious' stamped all over it – but in this crazy year of crazy impulsive decisions, I had just made the craziest impulsive decision ever. In my defence, all I can say is: 'It seemed like a good idea at the time.'

Two days later, having left Igeda sixty quid to make the arrangements – yes, just sixty pounds sterling to get married in an exotic Balinese village! – we duly turned up in Menyali. All the villagers were there, dozens of them, and they'd brought an old blind priest on a donkey to perform the service. Nicky and I were crammed into impossibly tight Balinese clothing – we were obviously much better fed than the locals – and then they

popped a turban on my head and a bee-hive wig on hers. A
drum roll announced the arrival of the famous Menyali gamelan band, and we were on our way!

I don't remember much of what came after, it all happened
so fast. I do recall our faces being constantly daubed with rice
and incense, and I smile in recollection at having to jump over
a 'wedding hat' of vegetables for good luck, but then – as the
band built up to a fever pitch of cacophony and the surrounding jungle vibrated with the echo of their sound – we were
married!

The following day, as Nicky was being given her precious
gamelan lesson by the Menyali band leader, I was shown into a
small, cramped room – full of ancient rice-parchment scrolls –
and introduced to a small, serious man with horn-rimmed spectacles and the bushiest eyebrows I had ever seen. This was the
village astrologer, and he wanted to know both our birth dates,
so he could make a prognosis on the marriage. 'Ah yes,' said
Igeda as he slowly translated back to me. 'This man say, you

are so lucky! You will be happy together for full-life term –
congratulations!'

He couldn't have been more wrong.

Chapter 6

Java Jive

As I waved Nicky goodbye at Bali airport, I couldn't help feeling a tiny sense of relief. The past week had been *very* intense – when we were not making love (which was often), we were tearing about researching my guidebook, snorkelling in the clear, blue, transparent waters, and engaged in long, late-night discussions about our *real* wedding, which was to take place in August. Now, with my loved one suddenly gone, I relished the prospect of some time on my own – it would, after all, be my last 'bachelor' time for the rest of my life.

From Bali, I tore through Java like a knife through butter – covering 50/100 miles a day, stopping in one place just long enough to gather information before steaming off to the next. Malang, Solo and Yogyakarta sped by, and then I was on the ferry from Cilicap to Pangadaran. In Pangadaran at 6pm, I found the tourist office closed but my *becak* (bicycle rickshaw) driver drove me to a local travel agency which gave me everything I needed…with the bonus of a free bus out to Bandung the next morning. I was chanting for, and getting help from, all sorts of *shoten zenjin* (protective forces) like this, which was just as well since I was living at the cheapest level in £2/3 Javanese *losmen* and getting no more than four hours sleep a night.

The buses were getting worse. The further we moved away from the big cities, the more often they were late and over-crowded. It was on one such bus – a packed-to-the-hilt air-conditioned one with all the windows shut and everybody aboard smoking *kretak* (cinnamon) cigarettes – that I thought of Kevin. Yes, the jovial, ruddy-faced young Englishman I had shared similar bus journeys in India with four years before.

'What ho, Frank!' his familiar voice had boomed down the phone the previous Christmas. 'I'm coming down to see you!'

'Are you?' I'd said, surprised. 'What's the occasion?'

'The occasion is: I want to learn some of that chanting.'

I stared at the receiver. 'You want to become a Buddhist? Really? I mean, you travelled round India with me for three whole months and didn't show the slightest bit of interest.'

Kevin chuckled. 'Well, I'm interested now. You said I could have anything I wanted if I chanted for it, didn't you?'

I hesitated. This could go badly wrong.

'Yessss,' I said slowly. 'So what is it you want so badly?'

'A wife,' stated Kevin. 'I've decided that I want to get mar-ried.'

And Kevin had come down to see me and he'd slept on the floor in a sleeping bag and learnt all about chanting, and then he had gone home again to Lowestoft and become the most zealous kind of super-Buddhist going. He had gone to every meeting, attended every course and chanted for up to five hours a day. It was typical Kevin. And three months later, whether by Fate or karma or sheer bloody-minded determina-tion, his prayer had been answered – he had found somebody prepared to marry him.

'That's fantastic,' I congratulated him when he phoned me with the news. 'So, how's the chanting going?'

'It isn't,' he said impishly. 'I stopped the day I met Cheryl.'

'Really?' I said, rather nonplussed. 'Didn't you want to continue?'

'What for? I got what I wanted. But I tell you what, Frank, if I ever need another wife I'll start back up again!'

I grinned to myself, thinking of Kevin. He was such a character. But then, as the smoke from all those *kretak* cigarettes got too much and our driver wiped his eyes to stop them smarting, the bus hit a pothole in the road, the back wheels jackknifed up in the air, and we all nearly died.

There was a moment's silence as the bus swerved and then righted itself, and then the huddle of kids occupying the front seats burst out laughing. They had never had so much fun.

The next bus I took, the 2pm to Bogor which only turned up at 6pm, provided me with a wry smile. Soon after departure, we pulled into a tiny village and some 30 drink and snack vendors boarded the bus. They all had their little trays of refreshments (very reminiscent of the old-fashioned usherette in the cinema) and every tray sold *exactly* the same stuff: a couple of cigarettes, a few tubes of sweets, some little bags of peanuts and an assortment of fruit and drinks. And they went up and down the bus, one after another, asking each passenger in turn if they wanted anything. The funny thing was that by the time they had all got off, I was the only person on the bus who wasn't eating. They talked everybody into buying something!

But my smile didn't last long. Instead of making up lost time, this bus made incredibly long stops for (more) tea and snacks and crawled into Bogor five hours late. I didn't even unpack – just fell into a cheap guest house and slept like the dead.

I was developing a peculiar love-hate relationship with independent travel. I loved the buzz of hopping on a bus or a train and going somewhere different every day – 52 hours travel in just eight days! – but without the Trailfinders crew or Nicky to slow me down, my nerves were getting frayed. I just didn't seem to have an 'off' button – my restless nature wouldn't allow me to relax in any place for more time than it took to have a plate of *sate* and a rushed cup of coffee.

None of this really bothered me, though. 'If the next 40 days go as well as the last 60,' I told myself, 'this is going to be a pretty special guidebook!'

The lengths I was going to, to make this guidebook special were herculean. I was interviewing up to 20 or 30 people a day, and whilst the bread and butter information was coming from travel agencies and tourist offices the real meat in the sandwich was coming from other travellers – people who'd actually 'been there' and got the T-shirt, people I was sharing cheap digs and long boring bus journeys with. They were all keen to contribute what they knew and many of them became friends.

The one and only place I'd had to pay for information was Solo. With the tourist office shut and nowhere else to get what I needed, I was forced to give a shifty travel agent £45 in exchange for four *batik* paintings and two hours of juicy gossip that no other guidebook in the world would be privy to. I didn't mind, actually. The paintings were very beautiful, and I sold them back home for far more than I had paid for them!

*

Jakarta, my next port of call, had to be one of the least likeable cities in the world. It was hot, sticky, dirty, polluted, annoying and generally mind-numbing. There was also nothing (apart from a couple of poky museums) to see. As in Kuala Lumpur, which Trailfinders had briefly called in on, they had ripped out what was mainly the old town and put an ugly heap of new buildings in its place. The only thing they had left unchanged was all the surrounding poverty. On the recommendation of Steve, who'd said 'If you want one photo that sums up Jakarta, this is the one!' I travelled down to the railway line below Slipi flyover. There was a *kampong* (village) here along both sides of the track and very dramatic it was too – a heaving slum of penniless destitutes framed against a glittering backdrop of high-rise hotels and business blocks. I just stood there – mouth agape, and my camera hanging uselessly at my side – and watched the poverty moving up the line and into the wealth of the city.

But Jakarta wasn't all doom and gloom. I did get a little chuckle from the *New Straits Times:*

CONDOM FESTIVAL TO BE HELD IN JAKARTA

JAKARTA, Fri. – A condom festival will be held here over the weekend to encourage wider condom usage among Jakarta men to curb population growth. The Chairman of the FPA (Family Planning Association) said the public had so far given 'encouraging response' to the festival which would consist of talks and distribution of condoms.

He said prizes would be given to winners at the festival but declined to give details on how they would be selected.

I didn't want to travel through Jakarta by bus – I still remembered John's experience of losing his passport – but then, going through another kampong area to the north of the city, I had to. And nearly lost something far more embarrassing than a passport.

'What are you *doing?*' I said as someone on the bus tried to remove my trousers.

'I like them. I want them,' murmured the misty-eyed youth hunched at my heels. He was obviously on drugs.

'Well, you can't have them!' I said, giving him a very non-Buddhist kick. 'Go steal somebody else's trousers!'

It was my own fault, I suppose. I really shouldn't have been wearing a pair of smart, white trousers in such a poor part of town. But I had been scarred, very early on in my writing career, by an unpleasant experience in India.

I could still hear his voice…

'No allow!' said the bearded Sikh, blocking my entrance to the Taj InterContinental.

'What do you mean, "No allow?"' I'd protested hotly. It was my first week as a travel writer in India, I had been promised free five-star digs at the top hotel in Bombay, and I was in no mood for an argument.

'We do not allow hippies!' sniffed the guard. His lips were curled in a sneer.

'Hippies? What do you mean, "hippies"?'

The Sikh's eyes had travelled down my body, nodding in turn at the ragged scarf on my head, the sellotaped Lennon specs on my nose, the golden hoop on my left ear, and the crumpled 'Just say Yes' T-shirt below that.

Then he'd begun sniffing in earnest. And with good reason. I had just come off a long, hot, sweaty 24 hour bus journey from Gujarat – most of that time trying to wrestle a leper off of my lap – and I smelt like a well-laid turd.

The look of profound disgust in his eyes did it. With a grunt of displeasure, I'd swept him aside, plunged into the hotel's vast lobby, and howled – with all the anguish that two days of no sleep and hardly any food could muster – 'I am *not* a hippy!

I am a *travel writer,* for God's sake!'

Fortunately, a nice PR lady had spotted me and called off the pursuing Sikh.

'There, there, Mister Queasy,' she'd said calmly. 'You'll feel better after a long, hot bath.'

'I don't want a long, hot bath!' I had raged, still quaking in her lobby. 'I want that man *sacked!'*

'We'll talk about that in the morning, Mister Queasy. Oh, and do me a small favour, will you? Lose the earring…'

That poor man. I really shouldn't have vented my spleen on him. He had only been doing his job. But how was I to know that in India you are what you wear, that most Indians will buy a suit ahead of a TV?

And it was the same right here in South-East Asia. If I wanted to write for the well-heeled, monied traveller, I was going to have to look like one.

Chapter 7

Marco Polo and the Voodoo Bus Driver

Sumatra was tough. To stay on schedule, I had to cover a country twice the size of the U.K. in just ten days…and on less than one hundred dollars.

Yes, that big, fat cheque Paula had handed me back in England was now half gone. I'd left the other half with my mum for safekeeping, but the thousand or so pounds I'd taken with me travelling was down to a few tattered notes. Forget a marriage in style with Nicky – I was now looking at a pauper's registry office ceremony and a cake from Sainsbury's.

Money aside, I was quite grateful to be out of Indonesia. Especially out of Jakarta. My only good experience there had been to be present when the Joju Gohonzon (special devotional scroll) was enshrined in the main temple. It had been an amazing ceremony.

I flew into Padang on the 4th of March. It was hot, hot, hot, and about to get much hotter. Someone had tipped me off about a great digs called Papa Chilli's Traveller's Lodge in Air Manis, but they had neglected to tell me of the total absence of transport to get there. I got a *dhokur* (horse-drawn cart) into Padang centre alright, but nothing prepared me for the long five kilometre walk – with 30 kilos of luggage, in the blistering heat – out to the lodge. It was gruelling! And I'd come on a Sunday, so had to run the gauntlet of irritating young students gawping and throwing nuts at the zoo-specimen foreigner.

I arrived at Papa Chilli's a steaming, melting mess, sweat dripping from every pore of my body. But the slog was worth it. The lodge was perched right above a beautiful, unspoilt beach, and while the great man was not there, his smiley son Ali, and even smilier daughter Yusna were. Sitting me down gently on the veranda, they fed me endless cups of tea and tasty *nasi goreng* until I got my will to live back again. That night, gazing out onto a magical sunset, I began to feel more optimistic about the upcoming Sumatran adventure. It wouldn't be that bad, would it?

Air Manis was geared to total relaxation. As Bob, Papa C's only other Western guest, related: 'Every day at 3pm, four brown cows walk down the beach in search of garbage and food. Around 4.30pm, the children vendors come by with banana, coconut and rice treats to carry you over to dinner. As the technicolor sunset light show begins, one dragonfly will buzz you continually if you sit on the beach. Soon after 6pm, a bat will fly random patterns between the boat and the palm stumps on the left. This will happen every day, but soon the days will cease to exist – just on and on and on, like the waves and the clouds, a continuum of change and "same same".'

It was tempting to stay longer and to test Bob's theory out, but I had no time for 'total relaxation' – the clock was ticking, and I had to move on…

*

The bus from Bukittingi up to Lake Toba, the popular travellers' hang-out at the centre of Sumatra should have taken twelve hours. It took twenty-two. The reason it took twenty-two was our voodoo driver, coupled with the most clapped out bus in existence. Half an hour out of Bukittingi, it ground to a stop, and instead of opening the bonnet to see what the problem might be, our voodoo driver – a short little man with a huge brush moustache and a ratty scarf wrapped round his head – just leant forward and began praying at it. At the dashboard, to be precise. And it worked! One click of the ignition key, and we were off again! But then, another hour down the line, the engine packed up once more. This time, no amount of urgent praying worked, so our voodoo driver resorted to stratagem two. He ripped the entire dashboard from its moorings, broke it in two over his knee, and tossed it out the window. And wow, that worked too, the engine purred back into life.

I was beginning to be impressed by our voodoo driver. It wouldn't have surprised me if he conjured loaves into fishes and water into wine. Okay, he was an unlikely Messiah, with his stubby cheroot hanging out of his mouth and his sweat-stained Bob Marley T-shirt, but I was prepared to believe.

I stopped believing thirty-two minutes later. That was when the bus coughed and died again. I watched as the voodoo driver ripped everything else out in his cab – pausing only to leave the gearstick, yes, he might need that – and then jumped out of the bus, a defeated man. But no, not quite defeated, he rounded up a group of old local ladies sitting by the side of the road, and got them to start praying at the bus while he went off for a snooze.

Two hours later, he returned, paid the old ladies some small gratuity – and a few packs of *kretak* cigarettes – and settled back into his cab. 'There is no way this bus is going to start again,' I thought to myself. 'He's dreaming.' But he wasn't. Miracle of miracles, holy of holies, the engine ignited with the very first click of the key and we were off again.

There was one other Western passenger on the bus, a mealy-mouthed American girl who refused any attempt at conversation – she wouldn't even give me her name. When the bus finally rolled into Toba, ten hours late, I watched for her reaction as she got off.

It was priceless.

'Well, goddamn,' she muttered darkly, giving one of the back wheels a vicious kick. 'I say *SHIT!*'

*

It was while sampling a delicious *martabak sayur* (vegetable spring roll) from a street cart *warung* in Bukittingi that I bumped into Steve from the Trailfinders tour.

'You look shattered, Frank,' he said with his familiar grin. 'Are you still burning the candle at both ends, "going off the beaten track"?'

'No, mate,' I said. 'I just got no sleep last night owing to an insomniac next door and a guy building a house right outside my window at 2am. What are you doing here, anyway?'

'Oh, I always come to Bukittingi between tours,' said the twinkle-eyed tour leader. 'It's got the cool hill-station air, it's got fantastic food like you're having right now, and it's got this ace clock tower in the square that looks just like Big Ben. It reminds me of home.'

I gave a wry smile. Yes, I had seen that clock tower earlier. It had reminded me of Nicky…and of how much I was missing her.

'Bukittingi also has lots of interesting little cafes which only close at midnight,' continued Steve. 'Look, there's one in particular that you got to put in your book – it's called The

Coffee House, and it's a real one-upmanship place, full of "real travellers" going on about who's done the most daring trip recently. Unless you've just crawled off a 60-hour horror bus from Yogya, you're ashamed to even sit down!'

'Oh, you mean the Marco Polo brigade,' I laughed. 'Yeah, I came across a lot of them in India. Their gig is to cover as much distance as possible in the shortest possible amount of time. A 40-hour journey across China, sleeping in a luggage rack, is bread and butter to them.'

'You should write a book about real travellers,' said Steve, flicking a stray mosquito from his close-cropped brown hair. 'I could give you lots of stories.'

But I didn't need Steve's stories. I found enough of my own in The Coffee House.

'How's it going?' I asked the waif-like young German girl sitting by the window. She was nursing a banana lassi. It looked like she'd been nursing it for hours.

'I am living on five dollars a day in Indonesia,' she intoned slowly.

Wow, that was impressive. I was having trouble getting by on ten. How was she doing it?

'Oh, I am eating at *warungs* all the time. I stay in the cheapest room in town, and I am not seeing very much.'

'Erm…why did you come here in the first place?' I asked, puzzled at her obvious lack of enjoyment.

'Oh, that is easy,' she said. 'I vont to say that I've come to Indonesia!'

Over in a corner, I saw two travellers in kaftans and funny ethnic hats having a heated debate as to who had had the most extreme travel experience.

'I've got malaria,' said the first guy. 'Look at the scabs on my arms and legs.'

'I've got guardia,' countered the second. 'I've been farting and shitting so long, I can't feel my arsehole no more.'

That annoyed the first guy, who now had to go one better.

'I got amoebic dysentery on a 36-hour bus journey to Kathmandu,' he said with a controlled hiss.

'That's nothing,' grinned the second guy. 'I had a six-month bout of hepatitis in the Himalayas.'

There followed a hilarious exchange which reminded me of the Four Yorkshire Men sketch from Monty Python.

'I spent a year in a Buddhist retreat in Manali, living on a bowl of rice a day.'

'I spent *two* years meditating in the Kashmiri mountains. Three grains of rice a day, that's all they gave me.'

'A rat ate my underpants in Pokhara.'

'An iguana bit me on the bum in Penang.'

'Right,' said the first guy, drawing himself up in his chair to put paid to the matter. 'I was swimming off the coast of Goa one day and a shark came along and bit off my leg. I had it sewn back on by a witch doctor, but he put these tiny little crabs in my ear that ate half my brain. Then, to top it all off, a bear bit off the back of my head in Dharamsala.'

There was a moment's pause as the other guy digested this information.

'Yeah, I *know* that bear, man,' he said at last. 'It ate my girl-friend back in '83.'

I grinned at Steve, and considered his idea about a book about real travellers. Then dismissed it. Not only would it offend about 90 per cent of people travelling to Asia (only the well-heeled travellers might get a kick out of it), but I couldn't imagine any of the subject audience forking out money to buy a copy.

'That's a pity,' said my chunky, weather-faced companion.

'But you're right. They're awfully keen on saving money...even when the cheapest option is not the best. Have you ever been to Pai in northern Thailand?'

'No,' I said. 'I was gutted when Ian didn't take us there. It's really off the beaten track, isn't it?'

'Not anymore,' said Steve. 'It's a typical freak centre now, with four guest houses. Three of them are awful bamboo-hut dives, riddled with spiders and vermin, and the fourth – which nobody goes to – is clean, quiet and friendly. In the morning, you'll find all the backpackers enthusing "Hey, this tarantula crawled all over me last night," or "I woke up with a rat in my mouth." And they just wouldn't listen to me when I told them of Duang Guest House (the clean one), even when I told them it was cheaper! It wasn't mentioned in their survival guidebook, so it had to be a rip-off. They much preferred the poky bamboo room with the paper-thin mattress, the rodents and crawlies, and the exhibitionist Dutch couple bonking away all night, clearly audible through the thin partitioned bamboo walls. "I couldn't sleep all night, man," was the classic complaint. "I was too busy listening...sorry, *meditating.*"'

Later on, having been up and down Bukittingi's many steep steps many times collecting information, I chanced upon Steve again.

'You're just in time,' he said, pulling me towards his hired motorbike.

'In time for what?'

'For something *very* different – the weekly big bullfight at Koto Baru. You won't want to miss this. It's not a blood sport, just a bit of fun.'

'As in a funny bullfight?'

'I think so,' beamed Steve. 'Two bulls lock horns in a muddy field until one runs away to fight another day. When the

48

loser makes his break, the field is suddenly full of zig-zagging locals going "Ay yay yay yay!" and having the time of their lives.'

Well, we went to Koto Baru, and I stood beside a bull to have my photograph taken, and the moment I took my hand off its back, it whipped round and nearly took my eye out with one of its horns.

'You shouldn't have done that, mate,' said Steve. 'That's one of the contesting bulls!'

Talking of bulls, the next day found me at Tuk Tuk on Samosir Island, overlooking Lake Toba. The rains had come, and I was looking over the lake from one of the island's traditional wooden *adat* houses with dwarf sized doors and large bull-horned shaped roofs.

It was an idyllic situation, and I should have been enjoying myself, but I wasn't. Heat and mosquitoes and long bus journeys had taken toll on my sleep, and I had become reliant on booze and Sominex to relax at night. Driven by a compulsion to work and to keep busy, I was now on constant hyper-drive, my mind buzzing away like a top.

'Why *am* I so restless?' I thought to myself as the shower drove a shimmering carpet of raindrops across the lake. 'What is it that is driving me on from one place to another, from one country to another, from one set of experiences to another? What's the hurry?'

I supposed it had to do with my father, who had died when I was two. A Polish immigrant lawyer who could not ply his trade because continental law was not recognised in England, he had died poor, frustrated and full of regret when he was just forty-four years old – working long and badly-paid shifts in a railway office. 'That's not going to happen to me,' I decided early on. 'I'm not going to have any regrets. I'm going to pack as much life experience in as possible in case I die young too!'

The other reason for my hurry was astrology. According to all reports, 35 was the most important year in a man's life – the year when he was supposed to shrug off the identity of his past existence on this planet and carve out a new one. I had been planning on how to do this for a long time – ever since travelling with Kevin, in fact. We had hurried round India at such break-neck speed, not stopping in any one place for more than a day or two, that I ingested more life experience in four months than I had done in the previous decade. 'Ah ha,' I thought at the time. 'Travel and writing, that's my new identity!'

But here I was, four years down the line, and I was so tired and wired, I was in danger of self-imploding.

Chapter 8

Big Blag in Kuala Lumpur

By the time I flew into Kuala Lumpur, I felt and smelt like a well-laid turd. Yes, the same as when I'd crawled off that leper bus in India a few years earlier, but this time much worse. Ten days of travel in the most basic of conditions in Sumatra had left me completely burnt out. I couldn't think straight, I couldn't even walk straight. Driven by desperation – 'One more night in a mosquito-infested backpacker hovel and I'll go mad! – I reeled out of the airport, staggered a few paces to the left, and barged into the office of the nearest travel agent.

The smart, coiffured lady behind the desk looked startled. 'Can I help you?'

I looked down, saw her name on the desk, and took a wild guess. 'Yes, Mrs Leng, is it? Where is Mr Leng?'

'He is in Singapore. Why, did you have an appointment?'

'Yes,' I said, giving every appearance of massive disappointment. 'Indeed, I did. I was supposed to meeting him *here* today. What's he doing in Singapore?'

'He got called away on urgent business,' apologised Mrs Leng, looking flustered. 'Can I help you?'

I hesitated. I'd pulled a few strokes in my time, but this was something else. It was in fact the biggest piece of bullshit I'd attempted in my entire life.

'Well,' I said at last. 'Mr Leng and I had an arrangement. My name is Frank Kusy and I am writing a new travel guidebook for the well-heeled business traveller in Malaysia. Mr Leng was supposed to be showing me around your beautiful city, and in return I was going to give your agency a full-page ad in my book and promote it to the hilt as the best one in K.L.'

'Oh, that sounds wonderful,' said Mrs Leng. 'Let me just phone my husband and let him know you are here.'

My heart stopped. If Mr Leng answered the phone, I was dead in the water. *'Nam myoho renge kyo, Nam myoho renge kyo,'* I chanted urgently in my head. *'Don't answer the phone, Don't answer the phone…'*

A minute passed, and then another, as Mrs Leng tried to reach the man with my life in his hands, and then she put down the phone.

'Typical lunch-time traffic,' she sniffed. 'All lines busy. But no worry, I will speak to him on his return. Now, please relax and take a glass of water. A.K. Travels will not let you down!'

And she was true to her word. Ten minutes later, a huge white limousine pulled up and I was whisked away to one of the top five-star hotels in the city. They even gave me a suit.

But as I lounged luxuriously in my sunken-bath jacuzzi and watched all the scum and filth of baseline Sumatra disappear down the plug-hole, I was not happy.

I had in fact not been happy since Nicky and I had parted ways in Bali. On our last night together, she had dropped a bombshell on me the size of Mount Bromo.

'I've got something to tell you,' she'd said, her eyes not meeting mine. 'I've had…erm…quite a few boyfriends before you.'

Well, this was a turn up. She was only twenty-four years old. How many could 'quite a few' be? So I asked her this, and she came back with 'Well, over forty as a matter of fact.'

My eyebrows soared. 'Forty?' I said incredulously. 'How is that possible?'

'It's possible because I was abused as a child. By my father. And then by his friends. I grew up thinking that the only way to get love and affection was to let men use my body. I'm sorry, Frank, I'm not proud of it, but that's the way it is. Or was. All I can promise you is the one thing that all those other men never took from me. A virgin womb. I've never been pregnant, thank God, so now I say to you: if you want our children as much as I do, you've got it. How does that sound?'

I wasn't sure how that sounded. I needed time to think. But even as she boarded her plane in Bali and I waved her goodbye, I'd felt this strange, fearful voice in the back of my head.

It was saying: 'I don't trust this woman.'

I felt horrible for thinking like this, I knew it was wrong, but as each day of my tour went by my sense of suspicion and paranoia had grown. 'She won't be able to wait six weeks. She'll get tired of me long before then. She bounced onto me on a whim – what's stopping her bouncing onto someone else?'

Now, with no word from her for over a month, I knew something was wrong.

*

Then, the very next day, I did hear from her. I got to K.L. post office at 10am, and found two letters waiting for me. One from Nicky, one from – of all people – Anna. The one from Nicky made several references to her ex-boyfriend Ian, whom she was spending a lot of time with, and hardly any reference to missing me. The one from Anna, by contrast, nearly made me cry:

'Losing you has made me appreciate just how precious to me you are. I am filled with a deep sense of absence – a numb, aching hollow inside, a small, locked room which will open again only on your return. Please, won't you come back to me?'

Maybe it was because I was far away in a foreign land, tired and lonely after so long without close human contact, but these two letters really confused me. I was starved for affection, I needed to be needed, that was the truth of it, and with Nicky being so strangely distant I was a hair breadths away from picking up a phone and calling Anna and patching things up with her.

But no, what was I thinking? That would have been crazy. I had already hurt Anna once. I would just go ahead and hurt her again, wouldn't I?

I had to face the sad fact. I didn't like being in love. It made me feel weak and vulnerable and out of control. For the first time in my life, I was not in control of my relationships – this girl, Nicky, had me by the gonads and was squeezing tight. Why was she being so cold and distant? Why were her few words so devoid of love and affection?

I began to dread going home.

*

Driven by worry and anxiety, I left the comfortable environs of K.L. behind and stepped up the pace. Having (finally) received some money from Paula, I thought 'blow the expense, no more torture buses for me!' and bought a £40 plane ticket over mainland Malaysia back to Singapore.

I was looking forward to exploring Singapore on my own. The previous visit, with Trailfinders, all I'd done was go shopping and hit a few bars and discos. Steve, already obsessed with Edie, hadn't even laid on a sightseeing tour of the island.

But Singapore and I didn't get on. First off, I accidentally dropped a sweet wrapper on its new, squeaky-clean subway and was immediately set upon to by three angry commuters demanding I pick it up again. Then I discovered that Bugis Street (where all the transvestites used to hang out) and Chinatown – the two sights I was most keen to see – had recently been demolished.

'The city is cleaning itself up,' a stern lady tourist officer told me. 'It is trying to discourage hippy visitors and to attract a 'better class' of foreign tourist.'

'That's all very well,' I replied, politely declining the deer's penis soup she wanted me to sample. 'But aren't you in danger of losing those well-heeled travellers who'll think the city is losing its character and who come precisely to see old Asian-style places like Chinatown?'

Her voice became snippy. 'Oh, tourists may *say* they don't want to see just skyscrapers and shopping complexes. But then they come here, get caught up in all the glitz of Orchard Road, do a day's shopping, take a quick organised island tour, and then they leave!'

I considered bringing up the sweet wrapper business, plus the fact that one of the Trailfinders crew had been thrown out of a high-class disco for wearing a pair of trainers (a brand new pair of Stan Smiths, mind you), but thought better of it. This lady, like Margaret Thatcher, was not for turning.

It was difficult, near impossible, to find anything off the beaten track in Singapore. 'Hmm, this is no good,' I thought as

I listlessly sipped on my Singapore Sling cocktail at Raffles Hotel. 'They've even closed the actual hotel for renovation. What's next for "improvement"?'

I was so depressed, I bought some 'Mighty, Loving and Happy Tablets' from a street vendor. The label said they were 'good for gentlemen whose nerves are not strong'.

My dismal mood lifted when I wandered into the area known as Little India. Here, I was instantly transported back to Delhi or Calcutta! The aroma of spices hung languorously in the air, small, wizened men in *dhotis* peered out at me from the dark interiors of narrow shops, and crimson blotches of betel nut juice stained the ground. 'This is more like it!' I rejoiced as I tucked into a delicious banana leaf meal. 'They haven't managed to ruin this place yet!'

My mood improved further when I came across a Bird Singing Concert at the junction of Sengpoh and Tiong Bahru roads. This featured rows of caged birds 'training their voices' while locals looked on over a breakfast of rice dumplings and strong black coffee. A madhouse of activity, the owners were constantly hopping up and down as they looked out the more experienced birds and moved their own younger birds next to them – to improve their voices, pick up new tunes and sometimes to compete. A good songbird, I learnt, could fetch up to £100…but it had to eat at least two grasshoppers, or two cockroaches, every day, or it wouldn't sing well!

That night, staying at the Why Not Homestead (Singapore's one and only hippy dormitory), I could have been singing pretty myself. I reached out, half asleep, to have a swig of beer from the bottle at my side…and downed a large, wriggling cockroach right along with it. There was a moment's pause as the surprised insect – which had been guzzling beer from the top of the bottle– made a brief appearance in my oesophagus, and then it was jettisoned, along with half the contents of my stomach, out again and onto the floor. Yuk, it took hours to get the taste of roach out of my mouth!

From Singapore, I burned up the east coast of Malaysia. I was expecting a lot from the east coast – not many travellers made their way here – but had to confess to being a little dis-appointed. The historic port of Malacca was well on its way to being 'beautified' like Singapore, Tioman Island was nothing like the idyllic Shangri La portrayed in the film *South Pacific* (I couldn't even find a cold beer) and the lure of Cherating – the opportunity to spend time with a typical Malay family in a fishing village – was gone when I found out the advances of the sea had washed the fishing village away. Okay, I found something good and positive to report on all these places (even on Cherating, which now had a new fishing village 5kms up the road), but my heart wasn't in it. My heart was back home with Nicky. 'What is it about this woman?' I thought to myself angrily. 'I've got to stop thinking about her!'

But I couldn't. My OCD was now operating at full pelt. It had been bad enough at the beginning of the year, when all I had to worry about were fluffs on the carpet. Now, I was ob-sessing about a much more troublesome 'piece of fluff' thou-sands of miles away on the other side of the world. And what was I getting in such a strop about? Well, Nicky was no beauty in the classical sense – her nose was a little too big, her chin a little too wide – but what she lacked in looks she certainly made up for in charisma. Witty, cheeky and funny, she had that indefinable 'it' which turned heads and had men walking into lamp-posts and falling off pavement stones. What was really worrying me was that when she drank too much – which she'd promised not to do in my absence – she wasn't responsible for her actions. Most of those boyfriends she'd told me about had wandered into her bedroom instead of a lamp post when she'd had a few drinks.

Nowadays, I could have resolved all my doubts with a quick email or a smartphone text. But there were no emails and smartphones back in '89. We didn't even have an answer phone in our small flat in London, so the few times I did hit a big city like K.L. that had an international call facility, I couldn't even leave a message.

And every time I did manage to get through, she was 'out'…

*

It was all very well my mentor, Daisaku Ikeda, saying 'The person who keeps moving ahead is eternally youthful, his heart is filled with flowers and shines brilliantly,' but I was so stressed out now, I had no choice. I didn't know how long I could keep it up, even whether I should be keeping it up. All that I knew was I *had* to keep moving! And it seemed to be working – the busier I got, the less time I had to brood about Nicky. Rantau Abang, Marang and Kuala Trengganu all flashed by in a trice, and then I came to Kota Bahru, close to the Thai border, and all of sudden something happened which stopped me in my tracks.

'You are travel writer?' exclaimed the happy little owner of the New Town Guest House. 'You no stay here. You stay my house!'

I surveyed the beaming figure before me. I had no reason to believe that he was going be an agent of torture.

'Okay,' I said. 'If that's not too much trouble?'

'No trouble,' he replied, still beaming. 'I am making one guest house for travellers. If you like, you can put in your book?'

Getting onto his small 50cc moped was tricky. My rucksack now weighed close to 40 pounds. But we eventually hauled it on board and puttered slowly out of town.

A long way out of town.

'Where are we going?' I began to silently panic. 'It looks like he lives in the jungle!'

And so he did. His 'house' was a hot, steamy, ramshackle shack perched right over a dank lake dangling with creepers and dense tropical foliage.

We talked for a bit, and his wife served up some palatable food, and then, around 9pm, he jumped up and showed me my room.

Actually, he didn't so much show me it – he practically shoved me into it. 'Have good sleep!' he said jollily, and re-tired for the night. I turned round to protest, but he had closed the door behind me. And locked it.

There was a moment's pause as I digested my new sur-roundings, and then shock horror set in. The room was small and dark – there wasn't even a candle – and it was alive with wildlife. It was bad enough in the gloom – I could only imag-ine where all the buzzing and chirping and slithering was com-ing from – but then I turned on my torch and it got a whole lot worse. Ants, cockroaches, and spiders were running up the walls, and the floor was alive with snakes and scuttling scorpi-ons. 'This is a guest house?' I thought incredulously. 'I've got to get out of here!' But my banging on the door and feverish cries for help were ignored. My host was either deaf or had left the building. So, shaking my legs about frantically to stop any-thing going up my trousers, I whipped out my trusty mosquito net, swept the bed clean of its carpet of creeping, crawling things, and dived under it, praying that there was nothing under the pillow.

'There is no way I am going to get any sleep tonight,' I thought, but in the end, I did. And opened my eyes to find a gigantic spider bouncing on the mosquito net, about an inch from my nose. 'Hello,' it seemed to be saying. 'Do you want to be friends?'

Well, no, I didn't. I had an uneasy relationship with spiders which went back to my childhood: at the tender age of four, one of the skin-crawling creatures had dropped down the back of my shirt from the ceiling. My mother had spent days calming me down. Then, a few years later, when we were staying in a boiler room 'flat' underneath an expensive hotel in Austria (it was all my mum could afford) I cut my knee while learning to swim and woke up the next morning to find a whole tribe of spiders feasting on the wound. That traumatised me for a lifetime.

'Wake now!' announced my host at 8am, jumping into my room and casually flicking the spider to the floor. 'Sleep more when dead!'

He didn't need to repeat himself.

I was out of that room in three seconds.

Chapter 9

How to get the Death Penalty in Malaysia

'Where is *stamp?*' said the angry little man, flicking through my passport and tossing it back at me. 'Why no *stamp?*'

I was standing at the Malaysian border, desperate to get into Thailand, and some idiotic border official was blocking my way. For what reason, I couldn't imagine.

'What stamp?' I said with a chirpy grin. 'Is there a problem?'

'Is there a problem?' he sneered at me dangerously. 'Oh yes, there is big problem. If you not get stamp come *in* our country, how can you get stamp to get *out*?'

He had a point. And light began to dawn. Ah ha, so this was Steve of Trailfinders' idea of a joke, was it? Letting all his crew get out of the bus when we entered Malaysia to have their passports stamped, and leaving me snoozing on the back seat? I wondered why he had that crafty smirk on his face when I woke up.

'So sorry,' I mumbled awkwardly. 'I…err…sleep on bus. Come into Malaysia sleeping, sleeping. Nobody tell me "Wakey, wakey, time for passport stamp." What can I do?'

The policeman pulled out his gun.

'You are illegal alien,' he declared, summoning another

fierce little man to his side. 'You know what is penalty for illegal alien?'

'No.'

'Death is penalty for illegal alien. You must come with us.'

The colour drained out of my face. *Death?* For falling asleep in the back of a bus? Could they be serious?

How serious they were soon became clear. I was led away in handcuffs and shoved rudely into a tiny, hot, humid holding cell with a noose hanging off the ceiling. Yes, a real noose. And as they took the cuffs off, one of them tugged the noose suggestively and ran a finger across his throat.

'Blimey,' I thought. 'They're going a bit over the top here. What's their beef?'

Two hours later, after my knees had gone numb from chanting, it came to me.

Ah ha, I thought, I must be paying for the sins of my original fore-father, Baron Kusy von Mukodel!

No, I wasn't crazy or imagining it, Baron Kusy von Mukodel had been a lot on my mind lately. Only a few months before, I had paid a trip to Krakow in Poland and the tour guide I had engaged to show me round the grand palace there had asked me my name.

'It's Kusy. Why?'

The guide's face went ashen. 'Don't tell anyone here this,' he said in a hushed whisper. 'They will kill you!'

'Oh, and why's that, then?' I said, amused. He was obviously pulling my leg.

'No, no, they will kill you, for sure. In 1596, the first Kusy, Wilhelm, tell King Sigismund to move his capital from Krakow to Warsaw. The king make a baron of him for his advice, but in one night the whole of Krakow lose half their business. The people of this town still call Kusy's 'blackbird' or the

Devil. That is the meaning of your name!'

'And they're still holding a 400 year old grudge? Are you joking?'

'I am not joking,' the guide said, in between showing me the miraculously well-preserved hand of some obscure martyr. 'They will take your blood.'

Well, by the rough way those Malaysian border policemen flung me in that cell, and the joy they took in confiscating my passport and pronouncing awful judgement, they were definitely after my blood. In fact, looking at their grim, unsmiling faces, they would have liked nothing better than to hang me from that noose on the ceiling and personally kick away the chair.

'Whoa,' I thought, 'they must be reincarnations of those disgruntled Krakowians. It's so obvious!'

My agony only turned to ecstasy three hours later, when – my knees having gone numb from chanting again – I stood up to peer through the barred window of my cell.

There, getting off another bus in the near distance, were a pair of bright-red plastic booties. '*Nobody* wears bright-red plastic booties in this heat,' I thought excitedly, 'It must be Rachel!'

And indeed it was Rachel, one of the girls on the same bus that had escorted me into Malaysia six weeks earlier. She heard my wailing cry for help, came over to identify me, and in two minutes flat my passport was both stamped into and out of the country.

'You were lucky, Frank,' she said with a laugh. 'I nearly wore sandals.'

Chapter 10

Love Shack

By the time I got to the idyllic little island of Koh Samui in Thailand, my dread concerning Nicky had turned to paranoia. Was she okay? Had she changed her mind about me? Didn't she want to get married anymore? These questions went round and round in my head, and drove me half crazy with worry and fear.

I was also one of the war-wounded. I'd torn an ear on a fence in Malacca and it had got infected, I was covered in mosquito bites from the one time I'd forgotten to spray myself at night, and the cold I'd contracted in Sumatra had gone to my chest and I was barking like a dog. How long could I keep this up, I wondered? Ten more places to see, and only 20 days to do it in. The clock was running…

On a tip, I made my way to Chaweng beach at the south of the island and checked into the small but friendly Moon Guest House. This comprised about a dozen shacks, crude and wooden and raised on stilts to keep out creepy-crawlies. The whole compound—built to put up the hippy backpacker crowd—was set just back from the beach in some kind of trop-ical rainforest.

Too tired after another week of baseline travel to think, let alone unpack, I flung my mosquito net down over my primitive Spartan bed and fell into a long, dreamless sleep. Six hours went by, and when I awoke at last, it was dark and the sound of wild cicadas was filling the air with a soothing drone. 'How wonderful,' I thought, transferring myself into the cosy hammock outside. 'I've finally found a piece of Paradise. I'm staying put here for a while!'

The guest house had a small café overlooking the beach, and the menu offered some truly tantalising snacks. I was particularly intrigued by the 'Magic Omelette', which had lots of shooting stars and grinning faces drawn in biro around it.

Just as sat down, a hand clapped round my shoulder and there was Nick, one of my old buddies from the Trailfinders tour. 'Hey Frank!' he enthused. 'I didn't expect to find you here!'

'Well, same goes for me,' I replied, getting up to give my long-lost pal a hug. 'Last I saw of you, you had a pile of snakes wrapped round your camcorder in Penang!'

'Yeah, that was weird. Little fuckers scared the bejasus out of me, what were they doing dropping out a ceiling anyway?'

'Hey, we got to celebrate!' I suggested brightly. 'How about sharing one of these omelettes? I think they got magic mushrooms in them!'

Nick looked at me dubiously a moment, and then broke out in a laugh. 'Okay, mate. Bring it on!'

An hour or so later, we were in hysterics. Well, I was anyway. Like all the other guest houses along the beach, ours had a 'Video Night' going on, and this evening's offering was *The Party,* starring Peter Sellers. The opening scene – with Sellers as an Indian bit-actor in a Raj-style movie who refuses to die (just keeps getting shot and coming back to life again and blowing his trumpet) – had me falling off my chair in parox-

ysms of laughter. Indeed, I was so stricken with mirth that I
rolled off the floor and into a ditch below the stilted cafe, and
had to be helped back up by one of the waiters. 'Blimey, those
omelettes are strong stuff!' I cackled madly, in between catching my breath. 'How long do they last?' The waiter looked at
me meaningfully. 'Sometimes you go up, sometimes you go
down, and sometimes you go up and never come down!'

I should have been panicked by this, but one more look at
the video screen, with Sellers giving one last forlorn toot on
his trumpet, and I was off again. And as I hugged my ribs with
uncontrollable hilarity, convinced that I had cracked at least
three of them, other guests from other beach bungalows, attracted by my braying laugh, began filtering into the café and
joined me on the floor. Yes, they'd all partaken of the local
shrooms too, and before long, the entire café floor was full of
writhing, wildly cackling, participants, all flailing their arms
and legs about like upturned beetles.

Finally, we all sobered up a bit, and I looked around for
Nick. But Nick was gone. Well, not quite gone, I eventually
spotted him way off in the distance…on a lilo. Yes, Nick wanted to paddle across eight miles of open sea to Koh Tao, the
neighbouring island, on a lilo! So I ran out to him on a local
motorboat, only to be shooed away by my still high-as-a-kite
friend. 'Leave me alone!' spluttered Nick as we dragged him to
safety. 'I can make it!'

The evening should have ended there, but it didn't. Still
buzzed up on psilocybinic chemicals, I went to a disco…

I normally hate discos, all that sweaty, frenetic pumping of
the air and pointless shouting at people for drinks and dances,
but this one – held in a small open field with lots of fairy lights
and a booming sound system – was different. Not only was I
still giggling like an idiot and imagining that everyone was

wearing pink underpants, but I somehow hooked up with a girl called Barbara, who seemed to find my antics amusing. 'Oh dear,' I found myself thinking through my hallucinogenic haze, 'I've got to watch it. My love life is complicated enough already!'

Barbara, or 'Babs', was a very smiley girl with masses of bouncy orange hair. I wanted to touch that hair, it was lovely and orange and bouncy bouncy, but I knew that if I did, it would open me up to a world full of trouble. Instead, I walked – or rather, stumbled – her back to her shack, which just happened to be right next to mine. 'Do you want to come in for a nightcap?' she asked sweetly and I summoned up every ounce of self-restraint and said, 'No, you're alright. Let's just have a chat on the veranda.'

The veranda was up a short flight of stairs to one side of the hut, and since there was only a single chair I made her sit in that and attempted some polite conversation.

'Did you see that film back there?' I giggled foolishly. 'The one they were showing in the field, on that piece of white cloth strung between two poles?'

'Oh, you mean the pornographic version of *Snow White and the Seven Dwarves*?' she giggled back. 'It didn't end well, did it?'

'Especially for Snow White.' And we both fell about laughing.

I wasn't laughing a few moments later. My left hand, which was resting against one of the veranda supports, had something cold and slimy crawling over it. I looked up and whoa, there was a big green snake staring back at me. I shook my head in case it was another mushroom hallucination, but no, wasn't. It was a fully grown python with black tattoos running all down its body. If I moved a muscle, it was going to bloody eat me.

'Are you sure you don't want to come in for a night-cap?' Babs said again, and all of a sudden, yes, I did, nothing would have made me happier than going in for a night-cap. But first, I had to wait for the king of snakes to wind over my arm and down the veranda post and finally set me free.

'Mind if I just finish my fag?' I said, trying to look cool and unconcerned. 'Go inside, I'll be with you in a minute.'

I breathed a sigh of relief as she got up and opened the door to her hut. I did *not* want her looking up and spotting that snake and freaking out. I wanted to keep that snake nice and quiet and untroubled.

But then she went and freaked out anyway.

'AAAAAR!' came her voice from inside the thin bamboo walls and I – ripping off the last few inches of sleepy snake – dashed in to see what appeared to be, in my altered state, a spider the size of a dinner-plate on her pillow. It was *enormous*, and my eyes bugged out of my head. How the hell did it get up those stilts? And what was it doing on her pillow— having a kip?

Terrified, Babs dashed into the toilet, and then dashed back out again.

'You won't believe this!' she shrieked. 'But there's a newly-hatched batch of baby *scorpions* running around in there!'

I thought and considered.

'You want to try out my place, then?'

'What's it like?'

'A lot safer than yours. And there's a double-sized mosquito net in there. We can both crawl under it and escape this horror-show.'

Later on, as she coiled her way round me like a *much* friendlier snake, and the flickering candle in our love shack slowly faded into darkness, I had a big smile on my face and a single thought in my head:

'I wonder if someone knows how to bottle those omelettes?'

*

It was only when I was in Australia that I realised I shouldn't be there.

Babs was mad. Quite mad. Having lured me away from the safety of my carefully planned itinerary – 'You can can spare a few days in Oz, can't you? We got beaches and barbies and beer and everything!' – my smiley, orange-curled temptress put me up in her pad in Sydney and revealed herself nuttier than a Snickers bar.

They say you can't escape your karma, that wherever you go in the world, you take it with you. Indeed, as my mentor Daisaku Ikeda once wrote: 'We can lose ourselves in romantic attachment, the euphoria is unlikely to last for long. As long as we remain unable to redress our own weaknesses, we will be miserable, no matter where or to whom we may take flight.'

Babs was the Polish biker chick again, but with bells on. Not only did she torment me with nightly barbecues – where all her friends talked about nothing but real estate and house prices – but every minute of the daytime she was on my case about joining some pyramid scheme into which she'd sunk all her money and which even an idiot could see was a blatant fraud. I tried to get away for a little 'me' time once, locking myself in the toilet to do a bit of my Buddhist chanting, but she unlocked it from the outside with a spare key and started dancing about in front of me, waving her arms about and screaming, 'You're here to see *me*. Not to do that rubbish!'

71

The final straw came when I went for a shower. 'Phew, at last,' I thought, 'a few minutes peace and quiet away from that loony person.' But no, I turned the tap on and a huge, black spider dropped down from the shower-head and landed on my left shoulder. 'OHH…MY…GOD!!' I shrieked as I scraped it off, and then 'WHAT…THE…FUCK!' as I noticed it was not alone. The whole shower was full of them.

Babs giggled as I fled into her arms. 'That's Henry,' she said, as Henry scuttled back up onto the shower-head. 'He likes it up there.'

'You keep a family of tarantulas in your shower?' I gasped, incredulous. 'And you give them names?'

'They're not tarantulas,' said Babs, a little irritated. 'That one on my pillow back at Samui was a tarantula, or something like it, that's why I was scared. These are Huntsman's, they're lovely, they're my little babies.'

Every inch of my body was crawling. I was sharing a hot, humid flat with a madwoman and about a dozen furry 'little babies'.

'Look,' I said. 'Either they go, or I do. Don't think me a pussy or anything, but ever since a kid I've had a thing about spiders. I even kept a plastic one the size of one of your little babies on my pillow at night, to scare away any real ones.'

'But they're not doing any harm,' protested Babs. 'They only come in to cool off in the shower. It's too hot for them out in the garden.'

It was a Mexican stand-off, and it was only broken when I grabbed up my towel again and went off for a swim. The swim was on Sydney's famous Bondi Beach, and I was looking forward to ticking off one thing on my bucket list – surfing a big wave on Bondi.

But, as with everything else about Australia (and this was

just tough luck), I was to be disappointed. I bobbed up and down on my body-board for six hours waiting for 'The Wave', but it never came and I dragged my sorry ass home again.

Here I found Babs, all dolled up and looking very nice. 'I've had a talk with Henry,' she said, 'and he's promised to not come in the bedroom if little diddums is scared of spiders. Though you'll have to be careful with Roger, he gets a bit upset if you step on him.'

'Who's Roger?'

'Oh, he's the family pet. My mum dropped him over earlier on.'

I looked in the bedroom and a sleepy, slit-eyed Roger stared back at me. A three foot Monitor lizard in the bedroom? I didn't think so.

*

'Paula? Paula? Can you hear me?'

'Yes Frank, how's it going?'

The line crackled. I prayed to Buddha it would not go dead.

'I'm in a real fix. Can you wire some money over?'

'Sure thing. Where shall I sent it?'

'Err, well, not Thailand.'

'What do you mean, not Thailand? Where are you!'

'Err, well, I met this girl. I'm in Australia.'

The phone went silent. I tapped it once or twice to make sure the connection was still there.

'My God, Frank,' said Paula at last. 'That's an awfully long way to go for a shag!'

It was no good telling her I hadn't had a shag – had in fact stopped just short of a shag out of respect for Nicky. She wouldn't have believed me. But she sent the money over anyway, bless her, and in a few short hours I was shot of Babs and her barbies and beaches forever.

Chapter 11

Stressed out in Samui

Back in Samui, I began doing what I should have been doing in the first place – touring the island by motorbike, picking up information as I went. Though once again I was distracted, this time by a van-load of happy Brits who thought I'd be better off with them. Several mud fights and bottles of Mekong whisky later, I was not so sure. And the van, which had started off pristine white, was now so caked in mud from the recent rains that it resembled an army camouflage jeep.

Later that evening, I made the acquaintance of a hilarious young Canadian called Dave, who had a never-ending stream of funny stories. Only that afternoon, for instance, he had been ensnared by a particularly clever Thai prostitute.

'Yeah,' he recounted. 'I'd been down to the beach, and my ears were blocked up from swimming. So I decided to visit a local doctor to have them syringed. Well, I was waiting at the bus-stop, and this very smart-looking Thai chick called me over. She had a map of Bangkok, and said she was going there in a few days and could I recommend a good hotel, since she was from Malaysia and would be kinda lost in the busy capital. So we chatted for a bit, and I happened to mention I was going to the doctor to have my ears syringed. "What luck!" she said.

"I'm a doctor actually!" I looked at her sideways and said, 'Oh, *are* you?' And she replied, 'Yes, I could make you feel *much* better!'"

Dave's crab dish looked nice and I asked him what it was. 'Oh, it's BARBECUED CRAP, it says so in the menu. I've had an awful lot of crap here, it's delicious. Here, you wanna try some?'

I shook my head dubiously. It was too dark to see. Maybe it wasn't crab after all.

'I tell you, man, you got to try stuff out here,' said Dave breezily. 'I go for the most outlandish dishes I can find. So far, I've had POTATO POO MARY in Delhi, PIG LEG IN HOT BOWEL SOUP in Bangkok, YUM BEAN in Kanchanaburi, and – my personal favourite – HORSE BALLS in Pattaya.'

I studied the red-cheeked youth with the lopsided grin before me. What was the son of a Californian surfer chick and a Canadian banker doing in Thailand?

'Oh, that's easy,' he said when I posed the question. 'I had to get out of India.'

'Why did you have to get out of India?'

'Well, I was up north in Manali, and one of those crazy street doctors gave me these foul-tasting black pills to cure my bad back. A couple of hours later, I started farting helplessly and it just *wouldn't stop!* I emptied the restaurant I was sitting in, no problem, and then my girlfriend left me because I stank out the room. This went on for *two days*, man, and people started crossing the road to avoid me. I was like this human pariah-dog with a red-raw arsehole and an aura of dead farts. Cured my back, though!'

I laughed, and fished around in my bag for a card.

'Yeah, I know those crazy street doctors in Manali,' I said. 'One of them tried to sell me a "love potion" with this endorsement:

This elixir benefits a man, can after use keep prolonged company with many a fair sex without feeling any sense of fatigue. He will have muscular energy like an elephant, he will be inflammable like fire, will have sweetness of voice like a peacock's, and will be noble like a horse. His treasure of human potential fluid will be added in plenty.

Dave gave a smirk, and then introduced me to his new bag, which he had just bought in Bangkok.

'You get a big bag like this,' he said, 'and you just wanna tell people about it. It's big. It's huge. You know, there are bags that hold a lot. And then there are BIG bags that hold everything, and there's still a little room left to throw other stuff in.'

'You like it, then?' I teased him.

'Like it?' enthused Dave, the surfer dude in him overcoming his earlier more 'bankerly' persona. 'I LOVE it. It's big. It's that big. And it's awesome, you know. It's big and it's awesome. It opens up into three sections, and I've still got a third capacity there – I can make it bigger still if I want to. I mean, God, it's half as big as I am now, and yet I've still got more capacity! It's not that I *want* to make it bigger, it's just that it has the POTENTIAL. If I want to, then I CAN. All other bags are nowhere. This bag is IT. This bag is the future. It is the future, right?'

I grinned to myself, and thought how nice it would be to travel on with someone like Dave. Innocent and naïve, ever-eager and curious, he reminded me of Kevin from my India days. But, as was so common with travellers on the road, he was going one way and I was going the other. We did the customary swapping of phone numbers and addresses, and thought we'd never see each other again.

We were wrong.

*

It was on the bus out of Samui – thinking that I'd pretty much covered the island – that I ran into Clifford.

'I get vibes about places,' said Clifford, his triple fat chins wobbling knowingly. 'I'm a lucky kind of a guy. I get instinctive vibes about places. I have my finger on the six pulses of the island. I can feel which energies are there and which aren't, and then I can apply the appropriate acupuncture to equalise them. What do you think of that?'

I didn't know what I thought about that. All that I knew was that I was sharing a six hour bus journey with a lunatic.

'So…err…what brought you to Thailand?'

'I HAD to come, man. I was so *stressed out* back home!' Clifford's huge bulk leant forward, emanating a powerful aroma of mixed sweat and alcohol. 'It's just the Western way of life, man,' he said. 'I mean, whenever you're in the West, you're in a job that you hate, you go home to a relationship that's not working *quite* right, *quite* right, and immediately, you're just *stressed out*, you know? You just can't get away from it – you're so *stressed out* all the time!'

I assumed a look of sympathy. 'Oh dear. What stresses you out the most?'

'Relationships,' said Clifford. 'I got these three Thai girl-friends – yes, three – and I'm trying to keep them all happy, but it's HARD, it's hard work, and sometimes I sit in my hut and I put back a bottle of whisky a day and I'm banging my head against the wall."

'It sounds like you're pretty stressed out over *here* as well!' I told him.

But Clifford wasn't listening. 'Yeah, you know, you've got to work HARD. You've got to give them – the ladies – a bit of dignity and a bit of space. You've got to forget the jealousies. I'm not a sexually jealous person. That destroys relationships!"

My look of sympathy was wilting. 'That's bullshit,' I told him. 'Why don't you stick to one girl and make her happy?

Clifford still wasn't listening. 'Jealousy is "negativeness", man,' he told me. 'I am only interested in positive vibes.'

It was alright for Clifford. Clifford was not a sexually jealous person. I was. Not a day went past now without me imagining Nicky in the arms of another man. I was particularly concerned about Ian, the most long-lasting of her ex's. In her last letter to me – the one I read with increasing anxiety – Nicky had hardly talked about anything *but* Ian.

'I've been helping Ian prune his roses,' read the pertinent passage. 'And I came across him one day up a ladder – he was refurbishing his conservatory. "Ian," I said. "If you fall off that ladder, can Frank and I have your house?" You could have knocked me sideways by his response. "Well", he said, "I ha-

79

ven't updated my will in five years, so by rights you still own half of my estate. I was rather hoping that if things didn't work out with you and Frank, you might come back to me." Ha ha, wasn't he funny?'

I didn't think he was funny at all. What was Ian doing sniffing round Nicky in my absence? And why had she made a joke of it, instead of rebutting him rudely? Ten thousand miles of distance was turning me into a green-eyed monster, with Ian firmly in my sights as a wily, two-faced, scheming Iago.

Chapter 12

It's my Job

Back in Bangkok, two pieces of correspondence were waiting for me. One of them was marked 'Urgent!'

'DON'T COME HOME YET!' screamed the telegram from Paula. 'IMPORTANT NEWS. CALL ME!'

Across the road was an international call centre. I went straight in.

'Something's come up, Frank,' my perky publisher told me when the connection went through. 'We're in negotiations with a big distributer in the States. They want a book on Thailand. They've ordered 10,000 advance copies!'

I blinked. 'Thailand? I've already done Thailand!'

'No, you haven't. You've done Bangkok, and a bit of the North, and a couple of southern islands. What about the rest of the North, and the West and the East?'

She had a point. The Trailfinders tour had been exceedingly lax in covering Thailand.

'But I want to go home!' I wailed. 'I haven't had a fresh pair of socks in three months!'

'Blow your socks,' said Paula matter-of-factly. 'This is an opportunity we can't afford to miss – that distributor is also taking 5000 copies of Bangkok to Bali. Look, I'll make you an offer that I've made no other author before, and probably won't do again. Ten grand advance. Take it or leave it.'

Ten thousand pounds? *Ten thousand pounds?* My mind was reeling.

'Err…I'll take it, Paula,' I said. 'That'll buy me an awful lot of socks.'

*

The only thing that stopped me dancing out the call centre and singing 'Hallelujah!' was the second piece of correspondence, which I now opened. It was from Nicky, and far from being all cool and distant – as I had been expecting – it was full or warmth and joy and excitement about my homecoming.

'My dearest Frank,' it read. *'I cannot WAIT until you come home. I am writing this in bed and imagining your arms around me and cuddling up to the small of my back. I've been imagining quite a few other things too, but seeing as the Sominex hasn't worked, if I start writing them down I shan't get any sleep at all, and it's 3.30am already!*

I can't begin to describe how desolate I felt when I had to leave you at Denpasar. The feelings manifested themselves as a physical pain, as if something had reached between my ribs with a claw-like hand and wrenched part of my chest away with its talon. I wept buckets on the plane to Jakarta, and I couldn't even feel embarrassed. I really didn't care what anybody thought – all I knew was half my life was still in Bali, and I felt like shit. You can forget facing nasty classes, mobs with bricks, killer horses or drunks with bottles – but to face leaving you for six weeks was the hardest thing of all. I don't know how we will do it Frank, but I'm NEVER going through that again.

Be sure that I think of you in all that I think, say and do, and I love you with my whole heart and soul (not to mention my naughty bits!) Take good care, my love – I can't wait to share my love, my life and my bed with you again. See you soon! Nicky xxxxxxxxx

p.s. I hope you get this letter. I didn't have the heart to tell you all this earlier because a) I missed you too much; b) I was very ill in hospital.'

I didn't think twice. I dashed back in the call centre.

'Hello? Nicky? Are you alright? I just read your letter. What's this about you being sick and in hospital?'

There was a pause as the airwaves struggled to connect us.

'Oh, what a lovely surprise, Frank!' Her voice sounded very small and timid. 'Yes, I didn't want to worry you, but I got sick right off the plane from Bali. I think I got bit by something in that beehive wig they gave me in Menyali. By the time I got to Heathrow, my guts had turned to water.'

'Is that why you didn't write me?' I said a little sulkily. 'You could have dropped me a line earlier, for God's sake! I was imagining all sorts of unpleasant scenarios.'

'Well, it didn't get much more unpleasant,' said Nicky, her voice turning snippy. 'I put off going to the doctor's for as long as I could, which was pretty silly of me, but then I collapsed in a recital I was giving for Mansell Bebb from the Philharmonic orchestra. Drugged up the eyeballs, and screaming with pain, I was whisked off in to an isolation ward in Tooting.'

'And?'

'And they found a huge mass of immovable tissue in my left side. Greg – you know dear Greg – asked me if I was having a baby! I didn't find this particularly funny and told him through gritted teeth that if I was, it'd be a bit small, so it'd better hang on till you came back cos I wasn't bloody having one without you. He grinned, and said "You two are gonna be *great* together!"'

I began to relax. Nicky still loved me. Everything was going to be alright.

'I'm so sorry, darling. So what was it, then?'

'What, the mass? Oh, the doc said it was a blockage or a kidney stone, and put me on penicillin. I've got a slight pain in my back even now, but hey, wink wink, I'm sure you can straighten that out. Only 22 hours to go, eh? Not long now!'

At this point, I wished I could back twenty minutes in time and take back my conversation with Paula.

'Welllll,' I said slowly. 'You're not going to like this. But something's come up. It's my job…'

It's my job.

What did I mean, 'It's my job?' I found myself reflecting on this as – with a heavy heart – I put the phone down on a very disappointed Nicky. What on earth had possessed me to sign up for yet another six-week jaunt round Asia when I should be hurtling back to my loved one after a hundred days in the wilderness?

The question was, what would I be hurtling back to? Okay, a few days of bliss and rapturous sex, but then what? All but a thousand pounds of my advance money for the Bangkok Bali book was gone, and in a few short months I would be penniless again. This new Thailand gig would set me up for a year – and (even Nicky had to accept this) give me the funds for our long awaited wedding.

'It's my job,' had however a much deeper and more worrying meaning. Ever since I had left university, I had found the standard 'nine to five' world of work impossible to function in. I was great at interviews – blagged my way into a number of employments for which I had little or no experience – but after the standard three month trial period I either got bored and wanted to move on, or I was sacked for sleeping on the job. On one famous occasion, I had tired of being an assistant branch manager of an insurance company in Cardiff, and had taken myself off – on the pretext of having some kind of super flu – to Ibiza on a Club 18 to 30 holiday. On my return, my manager summoned me into his office to enquire whether my health was now recovered. Upon being told that it was (with a hollow cough at my end to show that my life still hung in the balance), he had said, 'Yes, I thought so. You looked *very* well when you dropped your suitcase on my foot at the railway station yesterday.'

I had to face it, my job as a travel writer was the only work I was qualified for. It was not boring, I was my own boss, and I could go to sleep more or less whenever I wanted to. The song 'Wherever I lay my hat, that's my home,' could have been written for me. I really did not know where I would be the next day, let alone the next week, and that (for the most part) suited me fine.

What did not suit me fine however, was the emotional instability of my vagabond existence. This year, more than any other before or since, I was a pinball bouncing off whatever woman or romance that came my way. 'I want to be responsible,' I told myself. 'I want a settled relationship, maybe even marriage and kids.' But how could this happen when I was spending half the year on the other side of the world, thousands of miles away from the one person I had finally set my set my sights on – Nicky – and indulging my talent for irresponsible, unsettled living?

'It's my job,' was turning out to be more a curse than a blessing.

Chapter 13

The Unluckiest Man in the World

'You haven't met Bob?' said Dave incredulously. 'Bob's real famous round here. He's the unluckiest man in the world.'

I regarded Dave with suspicion. Dave was the gobby young Canadian I'd hooked up back in Samui – his outrageous statements were only matched by his outrageous sense of dress. Only that morning, he'd complained of 'this real weird look' some Thai woman had given him in a temple, and I'd snorted back 'What do you expect with a pair of orange underpants on your head? This is a temple, man. Not a beach!'

'No, seriously, Frank,' Dave urged me. 'You gotta meet Bob. He's a walking disaster. The only thing worse that could happen to Bob is to be dead. He's had bones broken, money taken, flights cancelled, friends leaving town with all his belongings – and not just once, but on several occasions!'

I sighed. When Dave was on one of his rolls, there was no denying him.

*

We found Bob nursing a banana milkshake in one of the quieter cafes in Bangkok's Koh-Sahn Road. He had a polka dot bandana round his head, and a small tattoo – of a snake – on the left nostril of his long, crooked nose. He looked like a sad, old dog which had lost its last bone.

'Oh, you got one of those banana milkshakes,' said Dave, drawing us both up a chair. 'I could have these milkshakes all day. At five baht, they're such a good deal. Go anywhere else, and they're ten or fifteen. Good call, Bob, these shakes are so good, the bananas are so ripe, they're just about perfect. And I should know, I've had a lot of them, I've had an awful lot of them!'

I shook Bob's hand and said, 'I hear you're the unluckiest man in the world. How unlucky is that?'

'Well,' sighed Bob, 'I arrived in Burma the day they de-monetarised the currency. All high value notes were declared illegal.'

'That was bad?'

'That was *very* bad. We were on a bus when it happened. All I had were big notes, and they were all useless. I had to sell all my film to survive. And my sleeping bag.'

'I don't believe this guy,' interrupted Dave. 'Over the past few months, he's been mugged outside a Wimpy bar in Sydney, had his jaw fractured in Bali, and lost his ticket to Singapore because the agent he bought it off didn't send it to him and absconded with the money.'

'Oh, and the day I moved into my apartment in Sydney,' added Bob, 'I believe the person with the key came back in again and stole my passport. '

I whistled. 'You're kidding!'

'No, a million things happened to me. I missed my bus in Kathmandu. That was the best one of all.'

'How did you do that?'

'I just didn't turn up in time.' Bob's laconic features

creased momentarily in a smile. 'But I think subconsciously I didn't want to catch it anyway. I'd found a much more interesting option: a special tour bus going to Goa. I really wanted to take this bus, because it was unusual. It was a bus full of German tourists. I wanted to take a three-week tour with them, because I thought it'd be a funny story – of an American on a German bus speaking only English. Unfortunately, I couldn't get enough material out of them. It wasn't as funny as I thought it'd be. Any one German on his own will speak a little English. But get them in a group, and they just speak German.'

'So for three weeks, you're stuck with this busload of Germans, and none of them says a word to you?'

Bob nodded sorrowfully.

'It was like living in Berlin.'

*

Later on, Dave and I went in search of a good Indian restaurant. We were fed up to the back teeth of Malaysian *nasi goreng* and Thai *khao pat*. No more 'nasty boring' and 'cow pat' for us, we decided. What we wanted was a nice, rich *rogan josh* or *jalfrezi* – the more greasy-in-*ghee*, the better.

On a hot tip, we travelled down to Silom area, looking for a place called Himali Cha-Cha. We had no trouble finding it either, because a huge billboard of the man himself – a grotesquely grinning and fat-faced Himali – set amongst a gallery of important personages he'd served down the years – blocked the entire pavement.

'Ooh,' I said, impressed. 'If even one of those royal testimonials is true, we're in for a treat. I'm already salivating!'

Upon entering, we found ourselves quite alone. Well, not quite alone – there was a huddle of Americans in a corner booth. And they were discussing the bread that had just come to the table.

'Whaddya think this is, Brad?' screeched one woman loudly.

'Well, I don't rightly know,' said Brad, scratching his head. 'What do *you* think, Emily?'

Emily touched the bread gingerly, moved it round the plate a bit, and then, after what seemed like an eternity, passed judgement. 'It's a NAAN! I know what it is! It's a NAAN!'

'Do you think so?' said the first lady. 'Oh yes, so it is! I would have cooked it less, and I'm not used to it being oval-shaped, I prefer my naan ROUND, but it's a GOOD naan nonetheless.'

'Your naans rock, Betty,' Emily reassured her. 'Especially the BUTTER naans. This is a PLAIN naan, we're not used to the PLAIN naans, are we?'

At this point, Brad beckoned Himali, the portly proprietor, to the table.

'Hey Himali,' he said with a braying laugh. 'Let's take a trip into the kitchen. You cook the naan, and I'll make the pizza!'

'What we need is *Caroline*,' piped up Betty. 'If *Caroline* was here, *she'd* know what to do. She'd tell this man how to cook naan!'

Himali was visibly moved. You could see that he had never been so insulted. Here he was, having personally cooked for Mountbatten and European royalty for forty years – and four jumped-up yuppies from Seattle were telling him how to make naan bread!

It was unforgivable, but he didn't let his famous grin slip from his face – he was heir to a long, long heritage of wearing ignorant colonials down by slow, Indian-style, attrition.

'Yes!' he said enigmatically, and went back to his kitchen.

Ten minutes passed…and then another ten. Then Himali returned to their table, still wearing his loony, toothy grin, and said, 'How is naan?' And they said, 'Fair,' and 'okay', but that wasn't good enough, so he asked them again. And again. And again.

Fifteen minutes later, Himali had quite worn them down. All four diners were now convinced that far from the naan being sub-standard or subject to improvement by Caroline, it was undeniably the best damn naan they'd ever tasted. They practically begged Himali to make them another one. Satisfied, he let them be, and the rest of their meal – which had gone quite cold by now – finally materialised.

*

The following day, Dave decided he wanted to be a famous travel journalist. 'It can't be that hard,' he grunted. 'Here, give me that Walkman.' And with that he slipped my trusty tape recorder over the table to a German backpacker who was sharing our digs at the TT Guest House.

'So,' he said. 'Have you got any good travel tips for a book that somebody might be writing?'

'Not so quick, please,' said the flustered German. 'I speak English not so well.'

'Okay.   Do…you…know…somewhere…good…to go…in…Bangkok?'

'No'.

'No?'

'Yes. The King's Palace. I think you must see the King's Palace.

'Yeah? Do you have to pay to get in?'

'Hundred baht.'

'Sorry. My tape recorder wasn't on. What was that again?'

'HUNDRED BAHT. Okay?'

'Okay,' Dave muttered into the microphone. 'King's Palace….must see it….hundred baht. Now, what is that?'

'It is my lemon juice.'

'Yeah? And how much is that?'

'Ten baht.'

'Alright…ten baht…lemon juice…this is the TT Guest House in Bangkok.'

'They write it on the bill.'

'Oh right…they write it on the *bill*…they write it on the bill at TT Guest House…good tip…examine the menu and look at the price before you have anything.'

'Why are you talking to your Walkman?' said the German.

'Oh, this is very important,' said Dave. 'I'm writing a travel book here. My name's Frank Kusy, actually. Maybe you've heard of me.'

'No.'

'Well, have you got any more good tips about the rest of Bangkok?

'No.'

'No good tips. Okay…Bangkok seems to be a total write-off, apart from the King's palace. Good tip, that. Good tip. Get the bus straight out of here.'

'You know,' said the German, looking pensive. 'It's very curious. I have been studying the label on this bottle of Mekong whisky, and the fruit on it looks just like our prime minister!'

'Right, got that. Helmut Kohl looks like a pear.'

'Ja! Everywhere in Germany, people know this cartoon of Spitting Image. And when you look at this bottle, it is the same! Here is the mouth, wide open. Here are the eyes. It is Helmut Kohl on the bottle.'

'OHHH! Chapter eighteen…mention Helmut Kohl and the Mekong bottle.'

The German's puzzlement deepened.

'I think this is not so important for a guide book?'

'What kind of sandwich is *that?*' said Dave, pointing at the German's plate.

'It is a chicken sandwich. Do you want to look inside?'

'Right…chicken sandwich…at TT Guest House…has onion, tomato and cucumber…and, oh yes, chicken. And how much is that?'

'I don't know. I think 25.'

'Twenty five baht,' Dave whispered into the mike. 'Possibly more.'

'I think again,' said the German, 'and King's Palace is too expensive. One hundred baht! You can eat four sandwiches for such much.'

'Note. Four sandwich! Quite so.'

'I prefer the sandwich.'

'Excuse me for asking, but why are you blowing your nose with your left hand? Is that a Thai custom?'

'You are always asking me something when I have something in my mouth,' spluttered the German. 'Can you wait until it is empty?'

'I'm sorry,' said Dave, switching off the Walkman. 'You've had your chance and you've blown it. I'm off to interview someone more interesting. Do you know Helmut Kohl's phone number?'

As the hapless German rose and left, muttering darkly to himself, Dave turned to me and said, 'I don't want to be a famous travel journalist anymore. That was a complete waste of time.'

'Yes,' I laughed, 'but at least I know how many sandwiches it costs to get into the King's Palace!'

Chapter 14

Off the Beaten Trek

The trek did not start well. I was bumpity bump bump bumping my way along a very bumpy 'road' with Dave, our new guide Swit, and two saffron-robed monks. One of the monks had a ghetto blaster pumping out Michael Jackson's *Thriller* into the jungle and the other one looked like he was about to be sick.

Suddenly, as the jeep rounded a particularly nasty bend, he was. And all the rest of us were covered in vomit.

So what was I up doing here? Why had I visited upon myself what was to be one of the most challenging weeks of my life?

The answer was simple. I was still gritting my teeth when I recalled that so-called 'trek' Trailfinders had laid on for me back in January. That last village we'd visited had been busier than a rush hour on a Friday afternoon at Piccadilly Circus.

I was also fed up of reading about such well-trodden trails in all the guidebooks. I was going 'off the beaten track' in mine – my readers were going to get something new and different!

To this end, I had engaged the services of a diminutive local guide called Swit.

I liked Swit. Thirty years old, and possessed of a mischievous grin which engaged me to him immediately, he was the most untypical Thai I had ever met. For one thing, he was not a Buddhist.

'You're a good Buddhist, aren't you, Swit?' I asked him jocularly, fully expecting a positive answer, and he gave me that mischievous grin and said, 'No. I am not pious. I am flexible. My dear papa was pious.'

As it turned out, Swit *had* been a Buddhist monk – a prerequisite for all Thai boys on their way to manhood – but only for one and a half months. He had then left the temple to pursue his dream, which was to become the best tour guide in Thailand. And what was the most important thing he had to learn to achieve this dream? He had to learn English. 'I have to learn English good,' he explained, 'because I am on the job. English is second language in Thai schools, but only reading and writing. So most Thais who finish from school cannot *speak* English.'

While he was telling me this, a beggar sidled up to us and started making strange parping sounds on a wooden mouth organ. 'What is the Thai attitude to begging?' I quizzed Swit. 'Is this man trying to make merit here?' My guide shot me that mischievous grin again. 'Some beg to live. Others are professionals, very rich. They come home to TV and all mod cons. They earn up to 200 baht per day. A few years ago in Bangkok, they caught a bunch of these professionals. The leader had a truck, and every morning he picked up ten or twenty beggars, and then dropped them all round town. Each beggar had his pitch, and if any other beggar tried to muscle in, there was a big fight!'

Dave liked Swit too. 'Man, but he's *short*, though,' remarked the chatty Canadian. 'I mean, I'm not tall and that dude doesn't even come up to my shoulders – I hope we don't lose him in the bush!'

By 'the bush', Dave meant the large, still remote, area north of Chiang Mai known as the Golden Triangle which had once been famous for its opium smugglers. Now, with the government burning all the opium fields and telling the farmers to grow vegetables instead, this area was ripe for tourism – the villagers had no other means of making ends meet.

But Swit did not want to go to the Golden Triangle. 'Weekend coming, too many Thai visitors,' he complained. 'We go north and west – first Mae Hong Son, then Pai. Look, there is a jeep with two Buddhist monks. Let us travel up with them…'

*

Half an hour off the jeep, a few clicks west of Mae Hong Son, we entered a beautiful old prehistoric forest. Everything was larger than life, like Conan Doyle's *The Lost World*. Massive banyan trees loomed up all around us, encrusted with fossils, and the air was alive with the cries and shrieks of baboons and wild birds.

'It is best,' said Swit, 'to be at the front of the line. Many leeches in forest. First person walk past, leech prick up their ears. Second person, leech on the move. Third or fourth person, leech get inside your shoe!'

I wished he hadn't told me that. Beforehand, I had been obsessing about spiders – wildly batting the little swagger stick Swit had given me against overhanging webs. Now I was dancing around, slapping my legs and squinting at my feet anxiously for leeches. 'Aaargh! It's got me!' I gave a strangled cry. 'It's squirming inside my boot!' But Swit was unsympathetic. 'You must walk faster,' he said sternly. 'Back of line is bad.'

'He's like the Yogi Coudoux, isn't he?' puffed Dave as our tiny guide skipped ahead. 'He's slowed his heartbeat down to 15 beats a minute and has entered some kind of mystic trance. Look at him go, and look at him veer off in different directions with every shift of his Yogi Coudoux mind!'

And it was true, because Swit appeared to have no idea of where he was going, but at the same time doggedly certain.

Three hours later, weary from slogging through the jungle, I gasped 'Where is the village?'

'Oh, one hour, two hour,' said Swit, slowing down to a trot. 'Local guide tell me "When you come to one dog, or maybe two dogs, you are near."'

Dave and I stopped to listen. Eventually, in the distance, we could hear three dogs barking.

'Is that it?' I cautiously enquired.

'Two dogs, three dogs, no difference,' sniffed Swit. 'We stop here!'

'Here' was a wide clearing with a scatter of ramshackle log cabins on stilts ranged around it. If this was a village, it looked like a pretty poor one.

How poor it was, and how little food it had, became apparent minutes after we arrived. I was sitting outside a hut, at the top of the stairs, looking over a beautiful sunset, when the lady of the house appeared and chucked a bucketful of slops over my shoulder. It landed in a big, deep hole which had been dug just below the hut. What happened next was unbelievable. I heard this thundering of footsteps, and a whole gang of pigs turned up and flung themselves into the pit. They fought over those slops like it was their last meal on earth, and the smaller ones – who couldn't get near the food – began shovelling up more earth with their tiny little tusks and eating it! The pigs were closely followed by a pack of wild dogs, who also jumped into the hole and began foraging. Roosters, hens, goats and a stray cow also made their way into the hole. The din was now quite incredible, what with a whole menagerie of live-stock trying to get in or out of that pit. The few slops were now long gone, and most of the animals were eating earth, literally digging and eating themselves into an early grave. Finally, just when I thought they'd never get out, a large water-buffalo showed up and flung himself into the hole. Everything else immediately vacated it.

Whoa, I thought, this is grim, what will *we* be getting to eat?

The answer to that question came shortly. I looked up and there was the village chieftain advancing on me with a wooden tray held high above his head. All the local children were run-ning around him, excited looks on their grubby little faces and screaming away like it was Christmas and New Year rolled into one.

'This looks good,' I remarked to Swit and the monk, who had both just turned up. 'I'm starving!'

I stopped being starving when the tray was lowered and our meal came into view.

What we had here were five toasted mice. Well, rather larg-er than mice, actually – three large, purple, hairy members of the *rattus norwegicus* family, looking like road kill. Their feral yellow teeth were bared in snarling defiance, and their tiny toasted hands were raised up in a gesture of reluctant surren-der.

The monk looked at Swit, and Swit looked at Dave and me, and both of us looked at the monk, and he looked back at us. Nobody wanted those mice. All three of us were waiting for someone to make a move.

At last, I did.

'Yum yum,' I thanked my host. 'But me Buddhist. No eat meat. Only vegetable.'

'Me too!' said Dave and Swit in unison.

The fat monk – who had been eating cheeseburgers all the way up, and who had indeed just given the chieftain the remains of his last Whopper – had no such excuse.

'Oh shit,' I could hear him thinking. 'Six months in this village and all I'm going to get to eat is toasted mouse.'

*

This Karen tribe village had been a find. We put it on our new trekking trail map, and moved on.

Though we soon wished we hadn't.

'Brrr!' said Dave, rubbing his hands together, 'It's cold!'

We were sitting in another Karen village just outside Mae Hong Son, the embers of the dying brick fire in our hut throwing out hardly enough heat to warm our toes. The sun had retreated from the surrounding forest, and we were looking at a very chilly night ahead indeed.

'Here,' I said. 'Have some of my blanket. I don't need it all.'

Dave's puckish features creased in amusement. 'No, you're alright. I got a thin, threadbare blanket of my own.'

Then his eyes alighted on a beaten tin can in the corner of the hut. 'Oh, what's that? Could it be kerosene?'

It was indeed kerosene, and as Dave picked it up I saw a devilish, excited glow in his eye.

'Yes, *this* is what we need,' he crowed. 'This is what the doctor ordered!'

Half the can sloshed onto the dying embers and the log fire

roared back into life again. Though 'roared' was an under-statement. It gave a titanic *PHWOOOSH* and Dave was blown back, his eyebrows singed clean off, to the back of the hut.

At the same moment, out of nowhere, the village headman came running in, his arms flapping all over the place, going *'Ay yay yay yay! Ay yay yay yay yay!'* Then he ran out again.

'Whoa,' said Dave, getting back to his feet, 'that was fun. He sounded like that video game *Bag Man* falling down a mineshaft. Let's have a repeat performance!'

And before I could stop him, he grabbed the kerosene and emptied the rest of the can over the fire. This time the blow-back was so powerful it blew the woolly cap off his head and gave him a permanent tan.

'Ay yay yay yay!' screamed the village headman, running in and out once more. *'Ay yay yay yay!'*

'This is too much fun,' chortled Dave. 'If I didn't want my eyebrows to grow back, I could keep this up forever!'

*

By day four of the trek, we were in a sorry state. We had been eating unspeakable stuff for days, and our boots were full of blood from leeches. Also, my hopes of virgin territory in the Karen tribes had been dashed when, in the last village we had visited, we had been cheerily greeted by a Frenchman in a hammock. 'Oui, homme!' he replied when I asked him if he'd been there long. 'It is nice and quiet and it is off the beaten track!'

'Bloomin' Frenchmen,' I observed to Dave. 'They always get everywhere first!'

Now, as we skirted the Burmese border and moved south towards Pai, we came to a Meo village without a Frenchman in it.

Even better, it had some rice.

'Oh right on,' enthused Dave. 'Some rice! Get a photo of that stuff! We got some rice happenin'! Give that man some matches for the fire. No, give him a lighter too! I'm so goddamn grateful for that rice!'

We watched as Swit mixed in the rice with boiled egg and chillies, and then, with gratitude bordering on reverence, we tucked in.

'That food was the best we've had on this trek!' I pronounced ten minutes later. 'Well done, Swit!'

'Yeah,' agreed Dave. 'It was awesome. You can tell the cook that.'

Just before our jeep arrived to take us back to Chiang Mai, we were treated to a cinema show. As in Koh Samui, the 'screen' was a thin white bed-sheet stretched between two bamboo poles in a jungle clearing. I picked my way through the gloom and plonked myself down on my ringside seat which was just a long plank balanced on two wooden stools. The film was *Rambo* with Stallone speaking (or rather, squeaking) in a hilarious, high-pitched Thai castrato, and near the end of it a vendor turned up offering little paper bags of 'snacks'. 'Ooh, mine taste nice,' I remarked to Dave. 'Just like Twiglets!' The two Meo kids seated either side of me were of the same opinion. They wanted my snack real bad. Quite a scuffle ensued as I fended off their prying hands, and then the film ended and the lights went on.

I looked down to see what those kids were so keen on.

I had dried cockroaches.

They only had dried beetles.

Chapter 15

How to Die in Khao Yai

Back in Chiang Mai, Dave did not hesitate. Throwing off his backpack, he flung himself into the hotel swimming pool and exclaimed, 'Man, I needed that!'

The water instantly turned a murky shade of grey.

I smiled as I watched my ebullient young friend from Canuck land splashing about in the water. It was so nice having a travelling companion once more, especially one with such endless energy and madcap humour. Bangkok to Bali, and Bali all the way back to Bangkok again, had been gruelling and lonely – I had met scores of people and made many friends, but none of them endured for longer than the time I had to move on again.

I also smiled as I recollected meeting up with Dave again a few days earlier. I had chanced upon him at a small café in Bangkok, which had had the temerity to give him only one nut in his chocolate nut sundae. 'So sorry,' the waiter had informed him. 'This not season for nuts.' Well, Dave hadn't liked that. 'Whaddya mean, this is not season for nuts?' he'd screamed. 'Next time, I'll bring my *own* nuts – this place is the pits!' I had had to reach over the counter and get him a second nut before he sparked off an international incident.

My smile began to slip with my next thought. Dave would be going home soon. His surfer chick mum and bankerly dad would be reunited with their perky prodigal son once more, and I would be left here alone in Thailand for three more weeks. It was not a happy prospect.

Before we embarked on our last set of adventures, however, I took Dave to task over something that had been bothering me for some time.

What is it about you and cockroaches?' I lectured him. 'Wherever we go, they seem to know you're coming and run out to meet you!'

'Tell me about it,' sighed my harassed young friend. 'I just had a wildlife experience in the shower.'

'Again?'

'Yeah, again. I get down to the shower, and I look around, and – you know those two cockroaches I killed last night, only one was still there. So I think, "Oh well, no problem," and I get in the shower, and hang my towel and shorts on the blue hook there, and I go to turn on the water. And all of a sudden, the place where I had my hands was cockroaches an inch and a half *long!* Scurrying around on the walls, burning down to the floor, smoking between my legs – it was *awful!* Meanwhile, I'm trying to smash them with the soap dish, and they're like moving and shifting from side to side, and then they dodge behind the squat toilet where I can't get at them. So I think "Phew, that's okay, they're gone." But they hadn't. I dipped my head under the shower for a little bit, and I get this feeling like I'm being *watched*. So I whip around, and they're coming *back* at me, going up the walls! I hit out with the soap dish, and beat them to the back of the room. Then I start washing my hair, and I'm just starting to settle down, and I feel this wiggling between my toes, and I look down, and there's a *gecko!* It's sitting there between my toes, sharing my shower!'

I laughed. 'Well, that'll teach you for wiping out countless roaches with your flip flop last night, won't it? Direct cause and effect, man!'

'You mean I should stop doing it?'

'I mean, every time you embark on your one-man mission to destroy every roach in Thailand, you damage the same foot – the right one – which the roach-killing flip flop came from. So far, we've had the exploding sink in Samui which fell off the wall when you laid your toothbrush on it – crushing one of your toes – and then we had you walking onto a pointed stake at the entrance to the King's Palace in Bangkok, crippling you for three days. Not to mention all the coral cuts you said you'd got in Koh Pee Pee.'

Dave stood back to ruminate.

'You may have a point,' he said at last. 'I'm using the *other* flip flop from now on!'

*

From Chiang Mai, Dave and I moved south by train to Ayutthya, home of the Thai kings before Bangkok became the capital. The place was quite denuded of tourists, we were surprised to find, but I did get my horoscope done.

'Oh, you get number 26!' said the wizened little priest, rattling some wooden sticks and studying them as they fell to the floor. 'It's not so good, you know. Buddha says you must get sick, you must lose a lot of money…'

Dave's braying laugh echoed around the small Chinese temple. 'Ha!' he declared. 'You die a slow, painful death on November 26th!'

The diminutive astrologer ignored him. 'You must be careful around yourself!' he continued sternly. 'Too much of the thinking! It's not so good for you, you know! But…what is this? Yes, you must marry two women at age 41. Then you will be very happy! For one year. Then, at age 42, one of them get jealous and shoot you in the head!'

Now, I knew this was rubbish, Dave and I had a good laugh over it, but it made me think. Given my recent behaviour – going out with three women at the same time back in UK, my recent skirmish with Babs in Australia – I was quite capable of getting married to two women in the same year. And of getting shot in the head. Anna had proved that by nearly pushing me under that bullet train in Tokyo. The thing was – and this was an important realisation – all this time I had been worrying about Nicky, getting my knickers in a twist about not trusting her, when all along it had been myself I could not trust. My mother's words echoed in my ear: 'When *will* you grow up?'

*

Dave wasn't very happy when I insisted on a second trek, into the Khao Yai National Park.

'Oh, man,' he grumbled. 'Haven't we suffered enough?'

He had a point, so I gave him a little reward. Leaving Swit in the small frontier town of Chiang Rai, I hired us two 125cc Honda motorbikes and we roared off on in search of the Golden Triangle. We wanted to visit Mae Sai, which is as far north as Thailand goes before hitting the Burmese border, but the roads were negotiable only by jeep, not by motorbike, so we turned back and came to Mae Chan instead. 'Not much here,' said Dave, scanning the one main street and sleepy covered market. 'I wanna banana milkshake.' Well, he couldn't have one, I told him, but he could, if we got there, have a delicious campfire meal at the Akha Guest House halfway up Doi Tung Mountain.

We never made it. Even as we struggled up the hills east of Mae Chan, our bikes were beginning to fail. 'You don't see many cyclists round here, do you?' observed Dave as we got off and pushed up a particularly steep slope. But just then we did see one – a poor local farmer wearing a look of total despair.

A path to the left led away from the hills, and taking it we soon came to a |Kuomintang village – well, a Shan shantytown – only 3kms from the Burmese border. Here, we dined at the highest Chinese restaurant in the world and I decided to have my eyesight checked. I thought the lady owner was trying to sell me cotton socks. They turned out to be thick, ropey noodles!

Back down at Mae Chan, we forked north to Chiang Saen and then up to the tiny village of Ban Sop Ruak, which is the focal point of the Golden Triangle – the place where Thailand, Burma and Laos meet at the confluence of the Mae Khong and Ruak rivers.

'Is this it?' said Dave, clambering off his bike and surveying another one-bullock village. 'Where's the poppy fields and opium smugglers?'

'Yeah, I know, mate,' I told him. 'I was expecting more too. Let's see what's up this hill path behind the police booth…'

Fifteen minutes later found us standing in a small viewpoint pavilion looking over the confluence of the two rivers.

'Oh, so this is what it's all about,' said Dave, gazing across to Burma and Laos. 'Kinda cool, huh?'

Even cooler was the tiny hilltop temple we climbed up to from the pavilion. This crooked, crumbling structure was inhabited by an aged *maechee* or nun. I placed a few baht in her donation box, and she leapt up (well, as fast as an octogenarian nun could be said to leap) and thrust a small Buddha amulet into my hands. Then, a minute later, she returned with a banana.

I didn't think she got many donations.

'Hey, Frank,' said Dave as we prepared to leave. 'Check

out the awesome sign round the back of this temple!'

'*Ho! My God!*' said the awesome sign round the back of the temple. '*Sightseeing Ruin! Going be memorious, be trustful when Coming. Go forwards, not be Back. He who thinks himself wise, Oh Heaven! is a great fool!*'

*

'Are you ready to suffer again?' I asked Dave the following day.

'Bring it on, dude,' replied the ever-energetic Canadian. 'What's up next?'

Next was the Khao Yai National Park, a vast acreage of tropical jungle, dense forest, and green hills which supported all 195 of Thailand's species of protected wildlife. I couldn't wait to explore some of it: according to all reports, this was somewhere one could *really* go off the beaten track.

But then I went so much off the beaten track, I nearly died.

The first night was fun. Shortly after we moved into our primitive dormitory room at Ghong Ghaew, the rain came down in sheets. It transformed the forest into a dank, eerie swampland of dripping, ghostly creepers and damp foliage crawling with ants, leeches and molluscs. A spotlight was attached to our hire jeep and we went out elephant spotting. There were supposed to be 200 wild elephants roaming Khao Yai, but we didn't see one. What we did see, hiding under the tarpaulin on the jeep roof against the driving rain, were hundreds of species of moths attracted by the spotlight beam. 'Elephant go, moth come,' was Swit's summation, and we nodded at him sagely, as though he had just uttered some great wisdom.

The trouble about Khao Yai, and I only found out the next

day, was that while all the jungle trails were colour-coded – red-painted trees for Trail One, blue-painted trees for Trail Two etc – if you got lost and didn't go back to the last marked tree to try a different direction, you could plunge blindly on and disappear…forever.

'We go red path,' said Swit. 'Red path is good.'

'No,' I said contentiously. 'I don't want to go red path, everybody else going red path, I want to go blue path.'

Swit looked at me long and hard, and then shook his head. 'Too much rain. Blue path now big danger. I no go there.'

'Okay,' I said, pig-headed stubbornness in my voice. 'You go your way, I'll go mine. I'll catch you later.'

Dave's eyes flitted nervously between Swit and me. He was trying to decide between recklessness and safety. And for once, his sense of safety won the day. Shrugging apologetically, he turned his face from me and followed the agile little Thai guide to the next red-marked tree.

'This is *great!*' I silently exulted. 'Now I've got the whole park to myself. Blow Swit and his cowardly ways. I was fed up of following him all the time anyway!'

My joy turned to dread about half an hour later. Following the blue marked trees brought me back to the dormitory bungalow. I couldn't believe it. Even worse, the rickety wood bridge we'd come across to reach it the previous night had been washed away by the torrential rains. I could see the next blue-marked tree on the other side – all I had to do was reach it.

But pride comes before a fall, and a minute later I found myself wading thigh-deep through leech-infested rapids. 'This is no good,' I thought in panic. 'I've got to turn back!' But as I did so, I lost my footing and was swept along by the rushing waters to the edge of a raging, surging waterfall. My rucksack got snagged on a jagged branch – that saved my life – and I began screaming for help.

Suddenly, just as the strap of my rucksack began to give way, and my life really did flash before my eyes, a thin ray of sunlight pierced the dangling creepers like a sharp sword cutting through an ancient cloth of green. And there, as if by a miracle, stood Swit. 'This way!' he was calling as he summoned Dave to his side. And two minutes later, I was back on dry land, coughing my lungs out like a very noisy landed fish.

'How on earth did you find me?' I croaked gratefully, when I got some air back.

'We never lose you,' grinned Swit. 'I know you will die on blue path. We follow close behind.'

'Had enough "suffering", Frank?' quipped Dave. 'Man, oh man, that was exciting. Can we go again?'

*

The following evening, safely returned to Bangkok, Dave stormed into my room in a state of high agitation. He'd been wandering around the red-light area of Patpong, checking out fake Rolex watches, when he had somehow been lured into some gay hairdressers for a manicure.

'I shoulda figured something was wrong,' he complained bitterly. 'Because they made an *awful* job of my nails. They clipped off a bit here and a bit there, but their mind wasn't really on it. There was this one guy standing at the door, preening himself and playing with his hair, and he kept winking at me. After a while, he nods at the guy doing my nails and says to me, "He RIKE you! He RIKE you very much!" "Really?" I said, taken aback. "Well, that's nice. Tell him I like him too." This was obviously not the right thing to say, because the door guy comes over and plumps himself down and gets out this pot of Vaseline and starts rubbing this stuff into my fingers, massaging each one up and down with a wet cloth. "Vaseline!" he informed me meaningfully and I said "yeah, comes in handy, don't it?" Meanwhile, his friend had grabbed hold of my foot and was working on my toes, which I found pretty strange. But Mr Vaseline didn't find it strange at all. He just pointed at the foot guy and said: "He WANT you. He REDDY boy!" Well, I was out of there like a shot, man. That place was really *weird!*'

I laughed.'What's a reddy boy?'

'I dunno,' said Dave. 'But the Thai people kinda have problems with their r's and l's, so I guess he was trying to say *lady* boy, or transvestite. Whatever, it was a freaky experience. Cool, but freaky, you know?'

Chapter 16

Joss

'P_{ah}!' said Joss when I told her about my recent trekking experience. 'That is not a trek. That is a walk in the park. Let me tell you about a *real* trek!'

I knew enough about Joss to expect something spectacular. For one thing, her name was a complete misnomer – 'joss' meant lucky in Chinese but Joss was anything but lucky. She was in fact the clumsiest, unluckiest person I had ever met. Tall, big-boned and Dutch, she bounced around Asia like a chunky, happy-faced puppy-dog, attracting misfortune wherever she went.

Only the previous year, shortly after we'd first met and then parted ways in India, I had received a scrawled postcard from her. 'Dear Frank,' it read. 'Sorry if this hard to read. I am writing with my teeth. The rest of me is in traction. I go to sleep on bus to Kathmandu, fall off roof and down mountain. They bring me up by mule. Every bone in my body is broken, but I will be fine in few months. See you in Bangkok?'

Well, I had seen her in Bangkok, and had been amazed. Not only was she miraculously restored to rude good health – all her busted teeth replaced by shiny new caps, only a slight limp betraying her fractured hip and left leg – but her previously

112

manic energy seemed to have doubled. 'Let us do Patpong!' she suggested brightly, and dragged me off to Party Night in Bangkok's famous red light area. This did not go well. First she let loose a two inch cockroach from a matchbox in a packed transvestite cabaret – 'Ha ha, look at everyone running to and fro – that is so funny!' Then she decided to become a pole dancer.

'I can do that,' sniffed Joss dismissively, as she watched all the bored Thai girls swinging round poles in the aptly named Pussy Galore club. 'Nothing to it.' And with that she stripped off all her clothing, brushed aside the protestations of the frightened manager, and clambered heavily onto the stage. The doorman couldn't believe his luck. 'Come quick! Come quick!' he shouted through his megaphone. 'Dutch lady in the nude!'

Now Joss was back in Bangkok, and telling me about the worst trek in the world. It knocked my own jungle jaunts into a cocked hat.

'This was not a good trek,' she told me in her strange interpretation of English. 'First, we go onto elephants. There are two German ladies on one elephant, an old French guy on another elephant, and me on a third elephant. My elephant go crazy when I sit on him, I don't know why, maybe he doesn't like Dutch people. He run off into the jungle, stop to fill up with water, then spray it all over me. It is a very bad elephant. Next, we are going on river rafting, and the raft falls apart and the two German ladies fall in the rapids and nearly die. Oh, and the French guy is left hanging out of a tree. Then I think"'These are crazy people, I will go back to Chiang Mai on my own." But I do not know where Chiang Mai is. I am wandering through the jungle, sometime on my hands and knees, for two days and not a sign of one human being. Then I come to this village and ask: "Where is Chiang Mai?" and they say "over there'. But 'over there' is on the other side of a deep....how you say...ravine. And the only way across this ravine is a wooden seat which this village puts young girls in and then swings them over to the village on the other side. Then all the unmarried men of the other village line up and she has to choose one of them as a husband. "I must do this?" I say with long face, and they nod and say "Yes. If you want go Chiang Mai, you must do this." So I get in the seat, praying that the rope will not snap and plunge me one thousand feet to my death, and point at some guy at the other side. He is very pleased to be chosen, starts making 'jiggy jig' motions with his fingers. Well, I don't want to make jiggy jig, he looks and smells like dirty buffalo, so I dope his drink with Valium and he go to sleep. After that, I run, walk, crawl for six hours more through the jungle...and come to Chiang Mai.'

There was a brief pause, as all twenty of so travellers dining around us digested this story, and then there was a hurried scraping of tables and chairs as they all rushed off to book the very same trek. Days later, the *Bangkok Times* was full of their stories: some had been thrown against trees by rogue elephants, others had been dashed against the rocks by disintegrating river rafts, and one or two had gone the full Monty and wandered into Laos by mistake and been kidnapped by bandits who held them hostage for big ransoms.

Joss was perplexed. 'Why these stupid people go on this stupid trek? Do they want to die?'

'No,' I said with a chuckle. 'They just want to get "off the beaten track."'

Chapter 17

Behind the Veil

The 16th of May 1989 will remain burned in my memory for a long time.

'This copy you've just sent me about the sex trade in Thailand,' Paula moaned down the phone, 'it's rubbish!'

'What do you mean, "rubbish"?' I retorted hotly. 'I've been up and down Patpong, Bangkok's red-light area, interviewing every "working girl" I could get my hands on. And that was bloody uncomfortable, since they invariably had their hands down my trousers.'

There was a pause and a sigh at the other end of the line.

'Well, it's not good enough,' concluded Paula. 'You say 70 per cent of Western tourists to Thailand are out there for the sex which they can't get back home. But is that a good thing to write about? Won't it hurt sales of the book if the other 30 per cent read it and think "Oh dear, I'm going to be surrounded by a load of pervs and sickos. I'm not leaving my hotel room!" I'm sorry Frank, but you're going to have to address this issue head-on. You're going to have to go in!'

My mind went into free fall. Was she saying what I thought she was saying?

"Go in?" I said, aghast. 'You mean you want me to have

sex with a prostitute?'

'That's exactly what I mean,' my prim and proper publisher told me. 'But don't quote me on it.'

*

Kanchanaburi was the last place I expected the dirty deed to take place. In fact, by time I had travelled half a day west here from Bangkok, I'd put the whole business out of my mind.

What was on my mind was the famous River Kwai bridge upon which the even more famous film starring Alec Guinness was based. Every Christmas, my stepfather and I, burying the jealousies which had plagued our relationship from the time my mother had first married him, watched rapt as Guinness fell upon the detonating device which blew the bridge to high heaven and sent the first train about to cross it plummeting to a watery grave.

To say I was underwhelmed when I got there would be an understatement. 'What?' I thought disappointedly. 'Is this it?' Instead of the rickety, trellised wooden bridge I'd seen in the film, there was a far neater and very boring-looking steel effort apparently made from odd-job materials brought over from Java.

But then I had a stroke of luck. Turning around, I saw the 10.23am steam train to Nam Tok coming up the line. Clickety clunk went the wheels, puffety puff went clouds of steam from the engine, and as the train slowed to a walking pace, there was a shrill 'Toot, toot!' from the whistle to alert non-passengers standing on the track. 'This is *fantastic!*' I thought. 'Blow the bridge, this is *exactly* the same kind of train as in the film – I've got to get on!' And as I jumped up and levered myself clumsily aboard, my happiness was made complete. From a nearby sentry point, a tinny tannoy started playing 'Colonel Bogey's March.'

Nobody seemed to mind that I hadn't paid my fare. They were far more concerned with the views, which were spectacular. Dense rain clouds rolled over the surrounding hump-back hills, slowly erasing them from sight – like a rubber erasing a pencilled landscape. As for the thrilling ride on the notorious Death Railway – so called because one Allied prisoner of the Japanese during WWII died for every sleeper they laid down on the track – well, my heart jumped into my mouth on two separate occasions. This was when the ground literally fell away from under train as it passed over yawning chasms on unsupported wooden sleepers.

Two hours down the line in Nam Tok, which was as far as the train went, I amused myself by climbing up an (empty) waterfall and looking for the elusive Cave of God. A local guy pointed out a 'divine' duck which was supposed to know the way, but although I respectfully asked it for directions, it just flapped its wings at me and gave a forlorn quack.

A much more interesting waterfall presented itself later that afternoon, when I took a bus out to Erawan. An idyllic spot with bags of multi-coloured butterflies and flocks of exotic birds, this had not just one, but seven gently cascading waterfalls, each with its self-contained 'swimming pool'. The biggest and best was near the bottom, but I couldn't understand it, everyone was just standing about in their shorts and swimming trunks.

'What's the deal here?' I quizzed a passing American. 'Why is no-one going in?'

'Well,' he said. 'I threw a sweet wrapper into the water earlier, and a swarm of piranhas gathered and munched it to pieces.'

'Piranhas?'

'Giant carp or catfish, I dunno which. Word is, lots of POWs from the nearby concentration camps were brought here during the war to have their gangrenous wounds "cleaned out". These fish kinda like human flesh.'

Just then, fortunately, a portly Japanese tourist turned up and wandered innocently into the pool.

'He's a goner,' said the American casually, and began whistling the theme to 'Jaws'.

There was a surprised yelp, then a frantic thrashing of limbs, as the poor Japanese attracted the attention of every nibbling fish in the pond and began fighting his way back to land.

Safe at last, the rest of us went in for a cool, refreshing dip.

*

Back at my small guest house on the edge of town, I found myself thinking again of what Paula had said – about paying for sex with a Thai prostitute. How was that going happen, I wondered, and how was that going to resonate with my Buddhist principles?

I didn't have to wonder long.

Walking past a strangely winking fat lady at reception, I found two British accountants having a beer in the lodge's little cafe. I wasn't going to join them at first – it had been a very long day – but then I overheard one of them telling the other that he was going to "buy him a girl" for his 21st birthday. My ears picked up. This sounded promising.

'Do you mind if I sit down for a bit?' I asked them. 'And what's this about buying girls – how do you plan on doing that?'

Well, nobody had to plan anything. As if by magic, just as I drew up a chair, three Thai girls appeared out of nowhere and started chatting us up. 'Hmm,' I thought. 'Maybe I'll let this happen. No way am I touching a girl in Bangkok, I've heard about all the nasty diseases, but I should be safe out here in the sticks, shouldn't I?'

Several beers later, the two lads filed away, each with a girl in tow, and I was left with the toothy one with a big grin called Chom. Chom was only 18, and obviously quite new to this game, but what she didn't know about sex was nobody's business. Back in my room, she ripped all my clothes off, sniffed and licked me all over (rural Thais apparently 'kiss' that way), and then started jumping my bones with enthusiasm. I felt sure she'd studied *The Joy of Sex* earlier, because she shunted me around into more positions than I've had hot breakfasts. It was a wonder to behold, and I was so caught up in the sheer balletics of it that I completely failed to…ahem…match her enthusiasm. Finally, having exhausted both herself and her entire erotic repertoire, she grabbed up her clothes and fled the building. 'Thank God!' I thought, relieved. 'I couldn't have kept that up another second!' So I leapt in the shower, to cool off all my sore bits, and thought the experience over. But it wasn't. A couple of minutes later, there was a loud banging on my door and I opened it to find....Chom, and two of her mates, holding a silver tray with four glasses and a bottle of Mekong whisky on it. All three of them nodding and smiling at me, and wanting to have a party.

The next morning I met up again with the other two guys. The younger one, Simon, Mister Birthday Boy, had had an even more embarrassing experience than me.

'I couldn't take my girl back to my room,' he confided,

'Bob, my mate, was in there with his. So I checked into the swank 5-star hotel opposite. All the staff stared at us as we walked through the lobby – "We know what you're doing!" I could hear them thinking – and then, to cap it all off, I found out my date was a virgin. And just as I did so, staring horrified at all the blood on the sheets, there was a knock at the door and upon opening it, I was confronted by a barber's quartet of room boys, towels folded neatly over their arms, singing "Happy birthday to you!"'

Chom was a nuisance. Despite me closing the door firmly in the face of her and her two chums, she trailed after me the whole of next day begging for presents and hinting heavily at a passport to the UK. 'What have you got me into?' I complained in a fax to Paula. 'I feel like a seedy cash cow!'

On a personal level, I'd found this experience both disconcerting and sad. Disconcerting, because I'd always associated sex with love, or at least with liking someone and making friends with them first. Making love to a total stranger was the most un-erotic experience of my life – how could so many Western visitors be getting off on it? Sad, because I knew a lot of these girls now – not just Chom, but a whole gallery of 'ping pong' artists and pole dancers I'd interviewed in Patpong – and behind their painted smiles there often lay a quiet desperation. Would they hook a rich *falang* and escape to the West before their age and looks let them down, or would they have to return to the incredibly poor villages of the North East where they came from and live out their lives in slog and drudgery?

Whatever, I had seen behind the veil of sex tourism in Thailand, and I hadn't liked it. Not one little bit.

Chapter 18

The Trouble with Trat

Koh Si Chiang, 50 clicks east of Bangkok, is quite the up-and-coming tourist destination nowadays. Back in 1989, it was virtually off the map. One dusty guest house, one dusty beach café selling luke-warm Kingfisher beer and nobody visiting except Thai weekend picnickers.

'What the hell are you doing here?' asked Jeremy, the kindly old Brit who was letting me stay on his yacht. 'Koh Si Chiang is deadsville!'

'Well, it won't be when I'm through with it,' I said confidently. 'And neither will Trat. I'm going on there next.'

Jeremy's face paled. 'Are you sure? Isn't that on the Cambodian border? '

'Yes, it is. Why, what have you heard?'

'Oh, nothing, nothing. Well…err…nothing good.'

I popped open another warm Kingfisher, and handed it to Jeremy.

'Don't worry, mate,' I assured him with a breezy grin. 'I have it on good authority that it's the next "happening" place. Virgin beaches, sea sports, and it's very own golf club. It's going to explode before too long, just you wait and see.'

Well, it was going to explode alright, just not in the way I was expecting. And I really should have known better. My 'good authority' was Steve, the Trailfinders boss who had stuffed me up at the Malaysian border. 'You bastard!' I'd accosted him back in Bangkok. 'You nearly got me the death penalty!' Steve had given his usual maddening grin and said, 'They wouldn't have held you long, mate, and anyway, you looked so peaceful sleeping on that bus I didn't have the heart to wake you up for a lousy passport stamp.' Then, as I'd continued my rant, he'd raised a hand and stopped me. 'Okay, okay, I owe you one. Look, have you checked out Trat? No other guidebook has covered it – it's off the beaten track!'

I'll never forget the sincere, conspiratorial look on his face as he bent down low to tell me this. He had no idea of what he was talking about of course, but he had me at 'off the beaten track.'

*

Back at Si Racha, the jump-off point for Si Chiang island, I was surprised to find no buses on to Trat. Well, there was one, but it left at midnight and I was keen to move on. 'If I get a nippy tuk-tuk,' I thought happily, 'I might slip in a round of golf before dark.'

Four hours later, all thoughts of golf were out of my mind forever. I was woken from my light snooze in the back of the tuk tuk by a light *thud...thud...thud* in the distance. Followed by a much louder *phtoom! phtoom! PHTOOM!* as we drew closer. 'Is this Trat?' I enquired of my driver, and he nodded and shot me a look of trepidation. Then, as we came into town – dodging through a maze of old wooden shop-houses and dark, narrow streets – he literally pushed me out of his vehicle and zoomed off again. His desperation to leave this place was breath-taking.

'Is this Trat?' I asked once more, this time of the ancient owner of a nearby guest house. 'And what is all this noise?'

'*Wheee...PHTOOM! Wheee...PHTOOM!*' The noise was getting louder. And closer.

'Sawadee-khrap,' said the old gentleman, dangling a key in my face. 'Ao hong mai?' (You want room?)

'*Wheeeee...PHTOOM...**PHTOOM!***' The walls of the guest house were shaking.

'Err...*put Angrit?*' (speak English?)

'Little...little...'

'What...is...this...noise?   What...is...this...PHTOOM! PHTOOM!'

The old man cackled between broken teeth.

'It is Thursday.'

'Thursday?'

'Thursday, Cambodia bomb us.'

'What?'

'*Mai pen rai.* No problem. Friday, we bomb them back.'

I was speechless. Trat was not an up-and-coming tourist Mecca. It was in fact a war zone.

My first instinct was to flee – missiles were now raining down from all directions, it was only a matter of time before one found me – but flee where and how? There were no vehicles on the road, there were in fact no people on the road. I stumbled out the guest house, desperately looking for some kind of safe haven, and found...a karaoke bar.

The karaoke bar was down one of the small, narrow, atmospheric sois which criss-crossed central Trat, and it doubled up as a bordello. Three hideously overweight women were dancing – or rather, lumbering – around poles on a raised stage, while in between them an even fatter Chinese-looking guy was attempting 'Don't be Cruel' by Elvis. It was the weirdest floor-show I had ever seen, and in my fascination I sat down and ordered a drink.

Well, that was a mistake. Before I knew it, two other heffa-lumps of women sat down either side of me and hemmed me in behind a table. Both were winking at me suggestively, and running their hands up and down my trousers. Then a waiter appeared with a menu, and before I had time to look at it, whipped it away again. A large bottle of expensive champagne appeared out of nowhere, and then a huge buffet of even more expensive-looking seafood.

PHTOOM! PHTOOM! Weeeeeeee...**PHTOOM!!!** The crash of exploding timber outside announced the death knoll of another nearby dwelling. I had to get out of here, and fast.

The size of the bill they laid on the table had my eyes standing out on stalks. But I didn't betray my feelings, I had to remain calm. 'Need _hongnam,_' I laughingly informed them as yet another bottle of champagne appeared. 'Too much water in tummy!' I exited the bar via the back door, giving the scummy toilet a moment's glance, and hit the ground running.

A passing tuk tuk was my passage to freedom, I threw my backpack on it and then myself and stuffed a 1000 baht note into the surprised driver's face. 'Bangkok!' I told him. 'And don't stop for anything!'

*

Back in the capital, I located Steve at his favourite haunt, the Whisky a Go Go bar in Soi Cowboy. 'You bastard!' I raged once again. 'I was going to write this section up as "Treat yourself to Trat," but all it is a mini-Vietnam. You should be ashamed of yourself sending me out there – I nearly got killed!'

Steve's maddening grin was never more maddening. 'You wanted to go off the beaten track, didn't you?' he smirked. 'I had heard rumours, but I didn't dare go there myself.'

Chapter 19

Big on Frogs

The phone rang at 4am.

'Mr Frank! Mr Frank!' said the voice urgently. 'Are you ready to go?'

'Go where?' I enquired, my head still half in la-la land.

'You must come quick! Meet me in the lobby!'

I was staying at the 4-star Swan Hotel in Silom, and this was my first attempt at a luxury sleep in two months. I did not want to go anywhere.

'Is that Steve from Trailfinders?'

'No, it is Mr Wong from Crispy Biscuit Limited. Don't you want to go to Cambodia?'

Well, no, I didn't want to go to Cambodia, I had only just nearly been there. As I slammed the phone down, I tried to remember, through my sleep-lagged brain, where I *did* want to go. Oh yes, it was Nakhon Ratchasima, otherwise known as Khorat. I wanted to catch the early 6.50am Rapid train there.

Though 'wanted' was perhaps not the right word.

I had to.

Four-star hotels don't come cheap: a whopping bill from the Swan had sent my eyebrows soaring. It came to half my remaining money, and no more was in the offing until Paula got her act together and wired some more cash over.

'I can't afford to stay another day in Bangkok,' I thought in panic. 'Oh, I know, I'll go hit the North East for a week – that'll be cheap.'

But money wasn't the only reason for my decision. I was also looking forward to *really* getting off the beaten track, in the poorest and least touristy part of Thailand. I'd had enough of chewing the fat with other western travellers – many of whom were content to just hang out in Bangkok or on the Southern beaches. This was my chance to write about and open up a region 99 per cent of them would never normally go to.

But when I arrived in Khorat, I had a shock. Nobody spoke any English. Walking down the high street, trying to get directions to the tourist office, I was met with giggles and blank stares. None of the guidebooks had warned me about this. It was like I'd landed on Mars without an interplanetary dictionary.

It hadn't been like this in Malaysia – most Malays and Chinese there both spoke and understood English quite well. And Indonesia had been a breeze – the Indonesian *bahasa* language was both simple and concise – hardly any tenses, with one word often taking in a whole phrase or sentence. 'It's like building blocks,' I'd told a doctor in Yogyakarta. 'You add little bits to turn adjectives into verbs and verbs into nouns. So *makan* (cat) becomes *makanan* (food) becomes *rumah makanan* (eating house).' As for Thailand, well, so much of it had been receiving Western visitors for so many years, I had assumed – in typical British fashion – that the whole country had at least a smattering of my language.

Right now in Khorat, I was being punished for my arrogance. About all the Thai I had was *Saweedee khrap* (Hello/Goodbye), *pom cheu* Frank (my name's Frank), and *mee hong nam?* (do you have a toilet?). I would have learnt more, but I'd been scarred by an unfortunate encounter with a bar girl in Bangkok. I'd tried to tell her she was very beautiful – *'Soway maak maak!'* – but had got the intonation wrong and wished her a lifetime of bad luck instead. Now I wished I'd persisted with my local lingo aspirations and began to curse myself for not bringing a Thai phrasebook.

Looking for somewhere to stay for the night, I checked into the imaginatively named *Khorat* on Assadang Rd…and then checked out again. Loud moans were emanating from the hotel's massage parlour, and there was a bizarre sign in every room saying 'No guests accepted with leprosy or other zymotic diseases.' I finally found refuge in the *Siri,* which had a 'prepare party place' (a roof with a view) and…oh, my lucky stars, a manager who spoke English.

'Where *is* the tourist office?' I quizzed him, 'I've been looking for it for hours!'

He laughed. 'We do not have a tourist office.'

'Oh, and why is that, then?'

'Because we have no tourists.'

How thin on the ground Western tourists were became evident the next day, when I gave up on the idea of seeing sights in Khorat (it didn't have any) and visited the atmospheric ruins of Phimai instead. Phimai, the hotel manager informed me, was Thailand's answer to Cambodia's Anghor Wat, so I expected it to be swarming with foreign tourists. Not so. He was right, there were no foreigners at all. Instead, I was surrounded by an army of inquisitive children who found me far more interesting than the ruins. 'This is amazing,' I thought, as they all jostled to touch and speak to me. 'I feel like Gulliver amongst the Lilliputs. And how friendly and welcoming they all are, how different to the jaded, painted smiles of Bangkok!'

It was at Phimai, courtesy of a chatty monk, that I made an important addition to my Thai vocabulary: *Mee manu neung kob mai krab* or 'I want some food with no frog in it.' Frog, I had discovered by now, was on every menu of every restaurant in the region. In Khorat, the Chinese style Seoy-Seoy near post office had not just FRIED FROG and SWEET BATTERED FROG, but even TOMATO SAUCE BAKED FROG. I took one look at the kitchen, which had skinned frogs floating about in a washing up bowl, and made a hasty exit.

There was a power cut that night, and I was plunged into darkness for hours, with only my torch and a book I'd already read twice to keep me amused. I looked around for the hotel manager but he had gone home to his own residence, which probably had a back-up generator. Boredom set in quickly, and with nothing else to do, I quaffed two Kingfishers and a Sominex and retired to bed early.

As I drifted fitfully off to dreamland, I had just one thought in my head: 'I'd kill for some interesting company.'

Well, I got interesting company alright. The next day found me on the 1.30pm bus out to Udorn Thani, sharing a seat with a local witch-doctor. This sinister-looking individual wore opaque shades, a set of pure gold teeth (he'd lost the originals in a motorbike accident), a chest full of tattoos, and strings of Buddha amulets adorning his neck and arms. Before I could stop him, he grabbed hold of my left hand and let out an ex-clamation of shock. 'Ah, you are Monkey Man – guru or crazy, I don't know, maybe you are both!' I gave him a shiny new one pence coin, which he wanted, and he gave me an ugly little black Buddha amulet, which I didn't. Then, for some reason, he took a shine to a photograph of my father, and when I wouldn't give him that, he got upset and whipped out his tarot cards and showed me the picture of Death. 'Why are you showing me that?' I asked him rather nervously, but he just grinned and turned his face to the window and didn't say a word the rest of the trip.

Trust the first English-speaking travelling companion I'd had in three days to put the willies up me. I'm not normally a superstitious person, but I'd seen a Sumatran voodoo driver resuscitate a dead bus – not just once, but several times. What had that witch doctor done to me? Had he seen my imminent demise? Had he placed a curse on me?

Fortunately, none of these things, because it was not me who died, but my Sony Walkman. As I made my tour of Udorn Thani's budget hotels, which were gross (one had a performing cockroach on the shower rail, another had a used condom sitting in the sink), I clicked on my trusty pocket tape recorder…and nothing happened.

'Oh my God,' I silently panicked. 'I'm in the middle of nowhere, with half the North East left to cover, and some spooky witch doctor has killed my Walkman!'

I shook it, and rattled it, and took the batteries out and replaced them with new ones, but still nothing. Then, in an act of desperation, I began praying at it. 'Oh pleeeese work again!' I told it. 'If you don't work, I'm going to have to write all my notes in long hand, and nobody, not even me, can read my handwriting!'

But that was only half the problem. My Walkman was not just a 5 x 4 inch piece of plastic. It was my constant companion. All those long, lonely bus journeys, all those even longer, lonelier nights in backpack hovels it had talked to me or soothed my mind with music. It would have entertained me the previous night too, had the batteries not run out. Okay, it was often just me I heard talking back to myself – accounts of the day gone past, perhaps, or funny/sad interviews I'd had with hotel staff or other travellers – but for months it had given me the illusion of having a best friend and without it I felt bereft and horribly alone.

My mood was glum when I took the two hour *songthaew* trip out to Ban Chiang the next day. Okay, so this prehistoric site had some of the oldest skeletons in the world, but so what? I couldn't report on it, so what was the point of going? Even the beautiful scenery – the colourful local fishermen wielding hand-operated Chinese nets, the lush paddy fields shimmering a glorious green – failed to move me. But then a beaming farmer got on and began proudly holding three muddy bags of fish in the air for everybody to poke and admire. That got a smile out of me. And as everyone else started smiling, I noticed the young saffron-robed monk in reflecting sunglasses happily grooving to U2 on his Toshiba ghetto-blaster. 'Fix Sony?' I said hopefully, and when he nodded shyly, I gave him my Walkman.

I don't know how he did it – maybe his magic was more powerful than the nasty witch doctor, or maybe his ghetto blaster had given him superior insight into Japanese technology – but one minute later he returned my precious word recorder to me in perfect working order, its little whirring wheels purring away like a contented kitten.

The first thing I did when I got my Walkman back was to whisper into it a warning not to share buses with local witch doctors...and not to show anyone in these parts a photograph of one's paternal relatives.

The second thing I did was to whisper into it something which I had just found in my Buddhist prayer bag. It was a quote from my mentor, Daisaku Ikeda, and it seemed particularly appropriate to my current circumstances:

The times when I have most intensely felt and experienced

the inner reality of creation have been those times when I have thrown myself wholeheartedly into a task, when I have carried through with that task to the very end. At such times, I experience a dramatically expanded sense of self. I can almost hear the victorious yell of victory issuing from the depths of my being.

Well, I wasn't quite there yet. My yell was still more of a subdued whimper. But after four months of travel, and two books nearly in the bag, I was on the home straight now.

I could almost see the finishing line…

Chapter 20

The Wackiest Wat

Nong Khai, the final destination on my whistle-stop tour of the North-East, turned out to be the best. Which was ironic since I had heard nothing good about the place, and had my eyes set on getting into Laos instead. I wanted to visit the famous Lao city of Vientiane, home of the revered Emerald Buddha, which was only 24 kilometres to the north of Nong Khai. Unfortunately, the Immigration Office near the pier was not encouraging. 'Can I go to Laos?' I asked one of the officers, and he said, 'Yes, but you no come back!'

So, I had to settle for spending a whole day in Nong Khai itself. Which turned out to be a good thing. A small, neat cheerful teacher called Prem adopted me as I was strolling down the road and insisted on taking me sightseeing on his motorbike.

I thought I'd seen enough temples for a lifetime, but no, I hadn't. There was one destined to restore my interest – and my sense of humour. Situated 5kms out of Nong Khai, Wat Khaek was surely the wackiest wat in the world, a fantastic Disneyland of bizarre and spectacular statues in the most incongruous of poses. Looking around me in the large open compound I saw towering, beak-nosed Buddhas, nightmarish *nagas*, eight-armed Kalis, and dogs wielding dinner forks and machine guns. All this reflecting the eclectic philosophy of a Brahmin *shaman* called Luang Pu, who had been driven here by the Communists twelve years earlier. And if I thought he'd already realised his triumph of the imagination, he was only just getting started. All round me more and more of these Easter Island-like statues were going up, the workers inspired by music and sermons from a blaring tannoy.

At the end of the building, I was introduced by Prem to Bhu Lua – the resident 'master'. It was hard to miss Bhu Lua. He was the guy wearing dark shades and dealing out tarot cards under a mountainous sound system. First he showed us round one of the weirdest collections of 'art' I'd ever come across – a two-storey 'shrine' choc-a-bloc with Hindu-Buddhist antiques and photos of Luang Pu. Then he introduced us to the giant catfish in the nearby lake.

These were no ordinary catfish. They were *huge*. And instead of throwing them one of the small bags of popcorn on sale at the picnic landing, I made the mistake of dropping in a large bun. There was a sudden, boiling surge of water, and a fully-grown catfish the size of a small shark nearly took off my finger.

Nong Khai may have been fun, but my feelings of elation were undercut by a sobering realisation: I had had enough of living on my own. Even as I said goodbye to Prem (what a nice man, he would accept nothing in return for his hospitality, seemed content just to practice his English on me) and trudged my way back to yet another lonely night at a guest house which doubled up as a knocking shop, I reflected that I hadn't seen a white face in five days. Even with my faithful Walkman safe and snug back in my pocket, I was beginning to crave Western company again.

But why was this? Why was I suddenly missing the company of my own kind when the people here were so curious and smiley and welcoming? Listening to a tape I'd made right at the beginning of my trip, when Hugo and Bridget all the rest of the Trailfinders gang were setting off to Chiang Mai – their cries of joy or despair filling the train carriage as they won or lost at Scrabble – made me think. I didn't particularly care for these people. I would probably never see any of them again. They were all just part of the temporary and very unique bond that travellers shared when on the road. Thousands of miles from home – away from all our loved ones, away from our comfort zone – we were all of us in that train as eager as each other to make relationships with people we could share our special experiences with.

This eagerness to meet with other travellers, I was also coming to realise, seemed to increase with the distance one got away from home. And also with the 'alien-ness' of the country one happened to be travelling in. I hadn't felt like this – been this desperate to meet other Western travellers – in Europe, or Israel, or even in Australia. But here in the outback of Thailand, where nobody spoke English and everybody looked different to me, I really did feel like an alien. It wasn't that I wanted to see white faces, I just wanted to see and meet somebody like *me*. Somebody who spoke and looked like me, and could relate to me, rather than look at me as a *farang* or a different species.

And just as I was ruminating on all this, someone turned up.

On the way to the Udomrot restaurant, I fell into exact step with a bearded German guy called Wolfgang. Born on the same day as Kevin from my India travels, Wolfgang had the same reckless fascination with the forbidden as did Kevin and nothing pleased him more than to find a track *off* the beaten track. We hit it off right from the start.

'Now, what shall we start with?' I said, as I surveyed the Udomrot's menu. 'How about FIVE THINGS SOUP IN FIREPAN? Or STEWED DEER GUT?'

'Ho, ho, ho,' roared Wolfgang. 'And then we can enjoy FRIED FROG CUTLETS and LUCKY DUCK as the main course!'

We settled on the Udomrot's speciality – 'Fried Mekong River Fish' which was advertised as 'fish you eat today, slept last night at the bottom of the river.' Since the restaurant was perched right on the river-bank, looking out to Laos, we felt pretty certain it could live up to its claim.

*

Wolfgang should have been on the early train back to Bangkok. It was quite a surprise to see him, much later on, on the late one.

'What are you doing here?' I said with a chuckle. 'I've had a whole day of touring temples. Did you change your mind and decide to see some too?'

Wolfgang looked sheepish. 'No,' he said. 'I got waylaid by Rama's Pastry House and had so many cakes, pastries and milk shakes, I completely forgot the time.'

The journey passed quickly, Wolfgang regaled me with eye-opening tales of his sexual misadventures in Bangkok. Then he showed me the two bags of 'earth from the banks of the Mekong' which he was taking home for a professor friend. We soon found ourselves in an empty compartment. That Mekong earth smelt like dog shit.

Off the train in Bangkok, I found myself famished. Seven

days of barbecued chicken and not much else had me holding my trousers up with one hand – I had lost so much weight! Leaving Wolfgang to his own devices – I still hadn't forgiven him for finding a pastry house in a region so big on frogs – I headed straight down to Ko Sahn Rd and packed away three American breakfasts in quick succession. I had a *lot* of eating to catch up on.

After that, and I was secretly dreading the result, it was time to hit the GPO to see if there was any news from Nicky.

Well, there was, but the three…ahem…'explicit' photographs that floated out of her letter had me blushing to my roots. Oh my word, did we really do *that* back in Bali? I hurriedly scooped them from the floor, hoping nobody else had seen them, and read the words I had been waiting for all this anxious time.

There weren't very many words to read, actually – just twelve.

'Dearest Ludwig,' said the letter. 'Just to remind you of what you've been missing. Nicky.'

Well, I guess I deserved that. I grinned on the outside at her impertinence – she knew I hated my middle name – but inside I still felt bad at cruelly dashing her hopes of a joyful reunion six weeks earlier. Those stupid words 'It's my job' were still ringing in my ears. I hoped she didn't have some kind of punishment lined up for me.

I had no idea.

Chapter 21

Back Home...to Trouble

Bangkok is a pretty clean city nowadays, but back in '89 – before it went lead-free and biodiesel – it was quite a different story. I returned to the capital to find smog and pollution hanging over it like a heavy blanket. The exhaust fumes of a million scooters, cars, motorbikes and *samlors* had clogged the early-morning atmosphere up with deadly, stifling fumes.

In amongst this, I spied an old man standing in the middle of the road, patiently waiting for the packed crush of traffic to part momentarily and allow him to wheel his small trolley – equipped with an umbrella, an assortment of fried foods, a teetering mountain of aluminium pots and pans, and two gently smoking tea kettles – to the opposite kerb. He waited, standing like some bemused gargoyle – his wide blue trousers flapping round spindly matchstick legs, huge white cotton shirt flapping around sunken chest, wide-brimmed coolie hat jammed tight over beak-like nose – for fifteen minutes under the sullen, smog-shrouded sun of Bangkok.

Behind him, manning the pavement, were two street salesmen. One sat in a hunched squat, vending two packs of Marlboro cigarettes, which were mounted on a wooden fruit box. They were still there, as was he, five hours later. The other hopeful, an eternally optimistic character, was manically winding up tiny toy monkeys and sending them cart-wheeling across the broken pavement stones. One of them fell down an open sewer. He seemed curiously unmoved. He wasn't doing any business either.

Out of the soupy haze came a shaven monk holding a flower and a begging bowl. He looked at me apologetically as if to say, 'Don't blame me for all this. I only live here.'

I looked to my left, and there was the city's first McDonalds opening up in Sukhumvit Road. I crossed over and shook Ronald's big, plastic outstretched hand. 'Welcome to Bangkok,' I told him. 'I think we'll be seeing a lot more of you.'

I guess I was sorry to be leaving the City of Angels – it had been a fun ride.

But by far the larger part of me was looking forward to going home…

*

My journey back to the U.K. was a nightmare – I never thought I'd make it. The plane failed to take off, we were stuck in a roach-infested 'five star' hotel for 32 hours, and my co-passenger on the plane we finally got had a bad reaction to his chicken korma and threw up in my lap.

But then, finally, after 138 days in the Southeast Asian wilderness, I stepped onto home soil again at Heathrow. And there she was at last…the love of my life, Nicky.

We hugged and embraced, and then we kissed…and I knew right away something was wrong. I couldn't put my finger on it, but something had changed. Something was different. There was a small, dark place in her heart that was closed to me now. I couldn't put my finger on it, but it was there…

*

'Who's Simon?' I said with suppressed fury as Nicky came in from work a few days later. 'What have you not been telling me?'

I watched as my loved one's face paled and then went white with shock.

'Simon? Which Simon?'

'Which Simon?' I echoed hollowly. 'The Simon you spent two hours with in a locked room at a party last month. Graham just told me about it.'

Graham was an old Buddhist friend of mine. We'd had a couple of beers earlier, and he had let slip this vital piece of information on an 'I think you ought to know' basis. I wished he hadn't.

Nicky's shoulders sagged and then began to convulse with huge, juddering sobs.

'OhGodohGodohGod!' she wailed. 'I knew I should have told you. But all the Buddhist women I confided in told me to say nothing. They said "How much do you love Frank? Do you really want to lose him?" And I honestly thought that if I told you, you'd do what any man would do and just up and leave. You wouldn't understand, I thought. You'd think "Oh, there goes Nicky again – leave her alone with a bottle of a booze and a man, and she'll do what she always did before you met her. Get her knickers off for a bit of love and affection." I'm so sorry Frank, I just couldn't risk that.'

I bit my lip and struggled hard to forgive those Buddhist women. I liked to think that if I'd known earlier, I could have been bigger than their assumptions of me. But in my heart of hearts, I knew they were right. The shock of discovery straight off a plane, after months of anticipation of seeing my loved one again, would have been too raw, too great. I would have walked out of Nicky's life forever.

'Well, maybe you should have,' I said with a degree of sympathy. 'Looks like I'm the last person in the world to know. What went on in that room?'

'It was horrible!' Nicky's tears ran in streams. 'I hadn't drunk a drop all that time you were away – well, maybe the odd glass of wine – but then you rang from Bangkok and told me you weren't coming home, that you'd taken that stupid second book on, and my heart just broke. That night, I thought "Sod it" and went to this party round Nina's place – she'd just got back together with Graham, and they were celebrating. I didn't mean to get pissed, I really didn't, but all of a sudden I felt myself passing out and Simon helped me up and into a spare room. How was I to know he'd lock the door and take advantage of me while I was crashed out on the bed?'

'He raped you?' I was appalled.

'Yes, and that's not the worst of it. He used no protection, and I'd come off the coil while you were away. So, a couple of weeks later – surprise, surprise – I found out I was pregnant.'

'*What?*'

Nicky staggered back to sit on the sofa. Mascara was running freely down her cheeks. She looked like a small and frightened panda.

'That's why I didn't write you in so long while you were away,' she blubbered. 'I had to have an abortion.'

'*What?*' I said again. This was turning into the wildest kind of sit com drama. You couldn't make it up.

'I'm so sorry, Frank.' Nicky was now snuffling into a hankie, her sobs dying away as she was overcome with exhaustion. 'It was the last thing I had to give you that no man had taken.

141

A virgin womb. And now I can't even give you that. Can you ever forgive me?'

I was conflicted. On the one hand, all my suspicions had been realised – she had been with another man. On the other, I had to believe that it had not been her fault – she had been used and abused by that scumbag Simon. The same scumbag Simon who had apparently fancied her for years, who had been bothering her non-stop while I was away with his lewd and suggestive comments. So, while very fibre of my being screamed 'Get out! This is what you've suspected for months, she can't be trusted!' the nobler part of me knew this was wrong. She had suffered far more than I. She had been bottling this up every hour of every day for the past six weeks. I was kicking myself now for taking on that bloody Thailand book. I had left her alone too long.

'Of course I forgive you,' I said, taking her in my arms. 'But there's one person I just can't forgive.'

*

I am not a violent person. I abhor violence. It's one of the main reasons I became a Buddhist. But a red haze descended over me then. Letting go of Nicky, I walked calmly up the hill to the pub, where I knew I would find Simon. And there he was, laughing with all his mates at the bar. He looked round and gave me a cheeky grin. I reached down and pulled his bar stool from under him. As he went crashing to the floor, I saw a glint of recognition in his eye.

'Yeah, that's right, you bastard,' I said. 'That's from Nicky and me. That's for fucking up our lives.'

Chapter 22

The Neighbours from Hell

The day I started writing my Bangkok to Bali book, the worst neighbours in the world moved in.

God, they were loud.

First, the television went on in the flat above us and began booming out an endless stream of soaps and game shows. Our banging on their door and broom handles to the ceiling elicited no response whatsoever.

Then came the bonking.

These two individuals had obviously not had sex for a long time. They went out (loudly) each night around 9pm, and came back (even more loudly) at 4 in the morning. Then they set to it with a will.

It sounded like a farmyard full of animals. Grunts, snorts, honks and blood-curdling howls suggestive of a wolf at bay floated down to us through the thin ceiling – punctuated by a high-pitched, sex-crazed narrative that had us jamming our pillows to our heads. 'Yes, yes, yes, YES! …No, no, not there, THERE! …Oh yes, that's it…Oh my God, oh my God, YESSSS!'

This nightly activity killed our own passion stone dead. We couldn't possibly hope to compete with it. And before too long, we were too stressed out and sleep lagged to even try. Nicky was given pills for her nerves by her doctor, and I began sleeping in the kitchen. Well, only my head was in the kitchen (it was a very small kitchen), the rest of me was still back in the bedroom.

Then, just as I was about to report them for aggravated social behaviour, it stopped.

The television went dead, the constant scraping of chairs above our heads came to a halt, and the torture bed which had woken us up every night for six long weeks bounced and sprang no more.

'Have they gone?' I enquired cautiously. 'What do you think happened there?'

'Oh, that's easy,' smirked Nicky, her perky, pink nose turned up in amusement. 'She must have wore the poor bastard out.'

*

Needless to say, I hadn't got very far with the Bangkok to Bali book. Let alone the one about Thailand.

'Where's my copy?' Paula shouted down the phone, and when I told her of the neighbour situation, she snapped back 'Are you a professional? Professionals always get their copy in on time. I was in Afghanistan as a field journalist when the bombs were going off and nobody got *any* sleep. I always got *my* copy in on time!'

It was no good telling her I'd have much rather been in Afghanistan, she would never have believed me. Instead, I bought myself an expensive golf-ball typewriter (state of the art in those days!) and set to work.

I had a big bag of tapes from my travels to transcribe. That was my first job. Then, having literally thousands of tiny snippets of information down on paper, I had to cut them all up (yes, this was before copy and paste on a computer) and reassemble them on the carpet. It was like the biggest jigsaw in the world – before too long, not one inch of the carpet was visible and even the kitchen floor was papered over.

'I can't live like this!' complained Nicky bitterly, 'I want my flat back!' But she was living with a man on a mission – with a near-impossible deadline to meet – and as the paper trail grew into a mountain and I started falling asleep with exhaustion at the typewriter, she started staying out at night…

*

It was three months later, in August, when I came out of my trance. I was happy. Paula was happy. The only person who was not happy was Nicky:

'If this is going to be our life together, with you "absent" half the year – either on the other side of the world or writing about being on the other side of the world – I don't like it. And where's our bloomin wedding? You've postponed it twice already!'

She had a point. But I was still waiting for the second half of my big advance from Paula. It would be a pretty poor wedding without that.

'Yes, I know, darling,' I reassured her. 'Let me just finish editing these final proofs and I'll phone Paula.'

But I didn't need to phone Paula. She phoned first. And what she said rocked my world.

'Hey Frank,' she greeted me. 'Have I called at a bad time?' I assured her that it wasn't, and then she said, 'Look, you better sit down. I've just had some unfortunate news.'

I knew Paula well enough to know that 'unfortunate' meant pretty much disastrous. I drew up a chair.

'I'm sorry, Frank,' she continued in an uncharacteristically hushed voice. 'But we can't pay you that second five grand advance on your royalties. That big distributor from the States has backed out.'

'*What?*' This was about as disastrous as it could get.

'Yes, I'm still furious about it. He seemed to think that we were putting colour pictures in your books – I don't know where he got that idea.'

'I had the same idea,' I said, slightly irritated. 'You know what I think of those cheap line drawings of cows and temples in my India guide. India is colour. Why do we have to portray it in black and white?'

My wily publisher sidestepped me. 'We're doing the best that we can!' she snapped. 'God help that you ever have to publish your own books! Have you any idea how much colour costs? If we put three sections of colour pics in, as that distributor wanted, it would jump the retail price of every book by two pounds…cutting our profit to practically zero.'

I hardly believed that, but let it pass. 'So what happens now?'

'What happens now is, we do a reduced print run on both books – say, 2000 each – and hope for the best.'

'*Hope for the best?*' I came off the phone in shock. With Paula in such obvious trouble and with no more guidebooks in the offing, my future as a travel writer looked grim.

There was no doubt about it. I needed a new direction.

Chapter 23

A New Direction

If I have to be grateful to Nicky for one thing, it was for starting me into business.

'I've just been listening on the radio about Margaret Thatcher's new Enterprise Allowance Scheme,' she said one day. 'It's supposed to encourage new businesses. You've done well selling those few trinkets you picked up in Thailand and Indonesia, haven't you? Why not try doing it on a larger scale?'

I blinked. 'Do you really think I could? I *hate* selling stuff, and I hate salesmen, but anything's better than sitting around waiting for another guidebook commission. Here I am, aged 35, and I've got five books in print but not enough money to pay the rent....let alone afford a wedding!'

In the back of my mind, I knew that Nicky's suggestion was a good one. I had no qualifications in business, had indeed failed Maths at school repeatedly, but, having been born into poverty, I had been making my own money since the age of six: trading rare pennies with geeks in mackintoshes, charming old men to take me into stamp auctions as their son, even swindling one-armed bandits at amusement arcades by memorising their complicated sequences. Yes, I was no stranger to making a profit.

And this was not the first time the subject of international trading had come up. Only the previous year, I had been sitting on the lawn of the Megh Niwas hotel in Jaipur when my old friend Colonel Fateh Singh – the jolly owner of that establishment – had broached the subject.

'You should try business, Frank,' he had chuckled. 'It would be a most spiritual experience!'

I had sniffed at the time. Spiritual experience? What was he talking about?

'I am talking about India,' he said airily, when I voiced my doubts. 'We Indians like to do business. It is in our blood. It is the key to our soul. It could be the key to your soul too, Frank. What have you to lose?'

Well, the answer to that question was now 'nothing'. I couldn't go back into Social Services – all the old people in my care in my last job had told me to get out while I could – and Nicky was right about the travel writing. One more guidebook could tear us apart.

*

They say that life has a plan for some people, that when they step out of their comfort zone and take a parachute leap of faith, someone turns up to take the jump with them.

So it was with me and Bernard.

September 12th 1989 saw both of us sitting in the waiting room of the Enterprise Allowance Scheme in Enfield. My mum had wanted to come, and so had Nicky, but I had put them both off, saying: 'It's about time I got responsible. I don't want anyone holding my hand.'

Then Bernard had reached over and offered his hand. It

seemed rude to refuse it.

'Hi,' he said, a shy smile crossing his dark brown features. 'I'm Bernard. Are you here to start a new business?'

'Yes, indeed,' I replied. 'I'm thinking of importing jewellery and handicrafts from India. How about you?'

Instead of letting go my hand, Bernard started pumping it furiously.

'Wow, that is a coincidence!' he crowed enthusiastically. 'That is exactly what I am planning to do also!'

I took in the madly grinning figure before me. Tall and thin, with huge buck teeth and a few strands of black hair combed over a balding pate, he looked just like Alec Guinness in *The Ladykillers.*

'I'm guessing you're from India?' I ventured. 'Have you family over here?'

'I am from Goa, which is the Portuguese part of India. And it is my family who is making me do this thing. I am 38 and still not married. My mother wants me to make some money and settle down.'

That sounded like a familiar story. My mother wanted exactly the same thing. And as we kept talking, a lot of other things in common came to light – we'd both worked in Social Services, we'd both worked in publishing, and – this was more than just a coincidence – we had both lived in the same street a few years before. But it was our common love of India, and of the Indian people, which really sparked our new friendship. By the time we got sent in for our interviews, we had already started planning a partnership together...

*

The first inkling I had that Bernard and I were not going to work out was when he missed our plane to India. The dodgy Indian travel agency he had booked the flight with had sold his seat to someone else. So I flew on alone, and waited…and waited…and waited for my new partner to turn up.

At 4.33am on my third day in Delhi, a dusty, beaming figure sprang into my hotel room. It was Bernard. After 22 hours in transit, he had finally arrived! He proceeded to tell me all about his flight and then, just as I came awake, he fell asleep. What a shit. I lay awake for three long hours while Bernard snored and grunted in brute slumber.

The second inkling I had that Bernard and I were not going to work out was when we started buying stuff. The idea was that we should pool our resources – three thousand pounds apiece – and take joint decisions on all purchases. That did not happen. First off, Bernard wanted to spend all his money first – 'I am going back to U.K ahead of you, I will get the ball rolling!' Secondly, he wanted to choose all his own stuff himself. My eyes rolled as he picked up, in quick succession, six marble chess sets from Agra, a dozen silver-plated tea services from Fatephur Sikri, and a big bag of cut gemstones from a dodgy-looking jeweller in Jaipur. 'God, I hope he knows what he is doing!' I thought to myself. 'Where on earth is he going to shift that stuff?'

My old pal Colonel Fateh Singh thought the same thing. 'Why are you making partners with this fellow, Frank?' he said. 'He has no idea of the English market!' But in my inexperience I had a kind of blind faith in Bernard. He said he had 'contacts' to sell to in London, and I was silly enough to believe him.

*

I stopped believing in Bernard about two weeks later. By this time, I had travelled the length and breadth of Rajasthan looking for stuff to buy, and was looking forward to going home.

One letter from Nicky changed all that:

'I phoned Bernard tonight – he has been mega-ill since his return but has struggled around trying to flog his gemstones, unfortunately to no avail. He says that most places only want uncut stones if they are high grade and that is too much of a risky business because you have to buy them by the kilo and cannot judge the quality. Anyway, he has a couple of places left to try so I'm chanting like buggery that he can get them shifted. He suggested maybe moving into silverware export and is waffling about doing all of this only for a hobby…you've gotta get back here and talk to that man!'

'Well, that sucks!' I thought. 'I knew he shouldn't have had that last curry at Delhi airport.' But the die had been cast, and they had fallen against me. Christmas was coming up fast, and if I had to have any chance of recouping our losses, I would have to get back to London as soon as possible. Christmas, I knew, was big business.

Business, however, was the last thing on my mind when I received that letter from Nicky.

The main thing on my mind was guilt.

They say in Japan that a man is not a man until he is forty. Before that age, he is still considered a boy – still subject to the whims of immaturity, still blown by the winds of passion and desire. And so it was with me.

I hadn't meant to fall in love with Maria.

It just happened.

Chapter 24

Maria

Maria came into my life just as I had finished most of my buying and had decided on a bit of R & R in Rajasthan. There was a small village called Khuri, way out in the Thar desert, close to the border of Pakistan, that I wanted to re-visit.

Call it Fate, call it karma, but sharing the small jeep bouncing out of Jaiselmer to Khuri was a small, blonde, breathtakingly beautiful Hungarian pop singer. This was Maria. She had read about Khuri in my India guidebook, she said, and had made it number one on her 'still to do' list before she returned home to Australia.

Oh, how we shrieked and laughed as our jeep juddered and bumped down one of the most inhospitable roads in India. Actually, for about half the 25 kilometre trip, there was no road at all – just a succession of dunes from recent sand storms. 'I feel like Rommel in North Africa!' I shouted over to Maria at one point. 'This is too much fun!'

God, it was good to have some Western company again. I was starved for it. Going off the beaten track was okay – I had, for example, just obtained a hoard of valuable Victorian silver rupees in a tribal village north of Bikaner – but I wasn't writing guidebooks anymore; I had no excuse to approach other travellers for advice and information. My new profession, I was discovering, was a very lonely one – night after night for two long weeks, I had sat by a dying log fire or a flickering candle flame in village huts or poor guest houses, going half spare in my isolation. Now, with someone to share my travels with, my angst and depression eased off, then faded away entirely.

Waiting for us in Khuri was my old friend Bhagwan Singh Sodha and his younger brother Tane. Bhagwan still wore the huge black beard for which he was instantly recognisable, and Tane, a resplendent saffron-coloured turban, which he said he had just used to bring up some water from one of the desert wells. It was five yards long!

Then we were welcomed by Mama Singh, a huge, generous presence who clasped me to her bosom as though I were a long-lost son. 'Good! You come again! Now you must eat!'

Mama's repasts were legendary. Ten courses of traditional breads and vegetarian dishes were laid out before us, along with endless cups of thirst-quenching cardamom tea.

'Is this all for us?' said Maria, her eyes popping out of her head.

'Yes,' I said, laughing. 'Bhagwan just told me, the number of tourists to his village has tripled in the last few weeks. I'm putting Khuri on the map!'

And it was true, because just one year before no western guidebook featured Khuri. They in fact wouldn't touch it with a bargepole. Even I, with my love of the 'off the beaten track', hesitated to go there. Military curfews, reports of violence, it was all very off-putting. But then I had met Bhagwan at the first fort gate of Jaiselmer – where he sat each morning in the dwindling hope of attracting tourists – and he had pooh poohed all these rumours and encouraged me to find the truth out for myself.

What I had found out was this: all the hotels in Jaiselmer had ganged up to blockade Khuri – they wanted all the tourist business for themselves. 'Khuri is restricted area,' they told travellers, or 'Khuri is in Pakistan', or even 'Khuri is out-of-bounds army post.'

Khuri was none of these things, I discovered. It was perfectly safe to visit. And what Khuri had was the one thing that Jaiselmer did not: mile upon mile of rolling, golden dunes for as far as the eye could see. Which made it ideal for the big camel trek into the Great Thar Desert that every traveller to this region craved.

Khuri was also the Western visitors' best chance of an authentic desert experience. 'If you can, spend a week or so here,' I told my readers. 'Learn about the people, and become part of their extended family and way of life. Here, you can really become one with the desert and its tribes!'

I had never, in the course of all my travels, stayed a week

anywhere myself – I was too restless a soul for that. But now, surrounded by the friendly Sodha family and with Maria as a warm and lively companion, I began to consider taking my own advice.

After a siesta to digest our massive lunch, Bhagwan and Tane took us for a tour of the village. It was dusk, the heat was down, and the desert sky was at its most beautiful – the thin cloud tissue burning a bright rose-pink before fading suddenly into darkness. 'Oh, it's just as I imagined it,' enthused Maria as we explored the small settlement of beehive dwellings painted with Aztec-like patterns. 'Look at the tough old village elders squatting outside their huts, pounding flax for wool! And there's some younger men and boys making bricks out of straw and mud for new dwellings!' Everywhere we went, the people of Khuri waved and smiled. They were genuinely pleased to see us.

Later on, after another mammoth meal and an excellent folk troupe music recital, we were shown to our 'special quarters', which was a private compound with two double huts. I generously donated Maria the hut with the single working oil lamp. Mine, it took me half an hour to find the toilet!

The next day, we went on our big camel trek into the desert. I knew what to expect, but for Maria it was a whole new experience. She hadn't even been on a horse before. 'You don't like getting up early, do you?' she'd said the previous night, suggesting that maybe we should call the whole thing off. That's when I realised she was scared. 'Look,' I'd comforted her. 'We can just go stroke the camels, if you like. You don't have to get on one.' But then I woke up in the morning and was concerned to find her gone. Had she had a panic attack? Had she got the first bus out of town? No, she had not. I reached the trek meeting point and there was Maria sitting on her camel, dolled up in a headscarf like a Tuareg, with a wide, loony grin on her face. She was so happy to have overcome her fear.

We set out at around 8am, when it was still relatively cool, and rode for about four hours, stopping at the most attractive dunes, until the heat became too intense round noon. Lunch, and a long siesta, was spent at a charming, unspoilt village, and then, around 4pm, we set out again. By now, we were used to the peculiar, rocking sensation of camel riding. Our kidneys had had a jolly good shuffle, and the slow, soothing desert pace of life had induced a deep sense of calm. I had never felt so at peace in my life.

The vista was a silent, empty yellow-white wasteland of rolling sands, interspersed with bare rock and desolate scrub. From time to time we saw a *chinkara* or desert gazelle springing across the flatlands, and on one occasion a flock of bright-plumed peacocks out for a stroll, but otherwise there was absolutely nothing out there. A few hours of this, and my mind went into freefall. I was five years old again and on my very first ride on the merry-go-round. I never wanted it to stop.

Camping out under the stars was fun. One of our camel drivers, Luk, flung us down on the ground, covered us with blankets, and told us to 'go sleep'. But then, all of a sudden, came the thunderstorm—a magical firework show of flashing lightning and dark rumbling clouds—and we had to hole up in a low concrete shelter in the middle of the desert. To keep us entertained, Maria sang some of the songs from her new album and everyone clapped enthusiastically. 'You sound just like Kate Bush, I complimented her. 'And if we could get you a wig, you'd look just like her too!

Everyone had hangovers the next morning, and had trouble waking up. But Luk had the answer to that. 'Jttt! *Jttt!*' he screamed at our camels as we boarded them and all of a sudden they broke into a galloping charge that had us whooping and screaming with exhilarated joy. 'What a buzz!' I called over to Maria. 'I feel like Lawrence of Arabia!'

Back in Khuri, we had a much-needed wash, changed into clean clothing, and prepared for another of Mama's enormous buffets. While we were waiting, we got onto the subject of music.

'It's impossible to avoid music in India,' I told Maria. 'It blares out at you from every roadside tannoy and chai-shop radio. You get on a bus, and you experience not just the songs, but the video of the film they came from. You board a train and everyone in your carriage bursts into an impromptu sing-along. You're waiting for a plane, and the whole departure lounge is awash with shrill female singing and manic tabla music. After a while, like most sounds in India, your mind reaches saturation point and blots it all out. Unless that is you come to enjoy it.'

As it happened, I had rather come to enjoy it, which made the appearance of Luk – and of a music tape of his choosing – both timely and welcome. 'This is desert *quwallies,*' he said with a sly smirk. 'Put in Walkman. I tell you what it mean.'

The reason for the sly smirk became evident as soon as the tape burst into song and the first chorus came up for translation. 'Ah yes,' giggled Luk. 'This is the marriage couple and they are talking about what happens at midnight in the bed. It is their honeymoon and the groom is saying: "Even nature is romantic. The sky is clear, the moon is high, the flowers are sweet and the breeze is light. The world has gone to sleep and we can go crazy." Then the bride is saying: "The light is off and my heart has become a campfire." Then the groom say: "It is midnight, the best time of night. It is many hours before dawn, so let us do something!"'

Luk listened a bit longer and then lapsed into hysterics. When he'd finally calmed down, I got the bride's final words on the subject:

'Time is passing,' he translated for her, 'and all you can do is TALK. You will do something or not? If you do every night like this, I will go home to my parents!'

Maria and I exchanged a look of concern. We would never view Indian music the same way again.

*

Little did I know it, but Maria had designs on me. Later that night, I spent an awkward couple of hours sitting on the side of her bed, chattering away about future travel plans while she regarded me strangely with those big blue eyes of hers. Then I retired to my room, somehow aware that I had missed something.

Which, of course, I had. Returning to her room fifteen minutes later, on the slim pretext of wanting to borrow her torch, I found her stark naked, except for a towel wrapped around her head.

'Frank,' she said quite casually. 'Would you like to sleep with me tonight?'

My eyes travelled hungrily up and down her lithe, boyish, ebony-white body. It seemed impolite to say 'No'.

*

Later on, as I lay in her arms, I was thinking. 'Oh dear, I've only known this girl a few days, but I could easily fall in love with her. What am I going to do about Nicky?'

Earlier that year, when I'd crashed into Barbara on a magic

mushroom omelette and lots of Mekong whisky in Thailand, I'd had an excuse for cheating on Nicky. Not only was I off my head on psilocybin chemicals, but I felt angry and betrayed at not having heard from her in so long. Now, as I brushed a stray hair from Maria's beautiful, gently sleeping, face, I had to accept that I had no excuse at all. Except that since Nicky's 'big reveal' about her pregnancy and abortion, she had become increasingly cold and distant. Maybe she believed that I could never forgive her, maybe she was having trouble forgiving herself, maybe it was just those long months of working on my guidebooks which had driven us apart. But every night of late, she had been 'out' with friends or family – I hardly saw her at all, we were like ships passing in the night.

'We're supposed to be getting married in four months,' I silently panicked. 'How is this going to pan out?'

It panned out rather well, actually. Maria wasn't too thrilled when I told her about Nicky, but I put it across in such a throwaway fashion – 'We've not been getting on for a while, wouldn't surprise me if she's moved out by the time I get home' – that she clasped me to her bosom and said: 'There, there, you've had a really hard time of it, haven't you? Why don't you come stay with me in Australia?'

Australia? Noooooo, I wasn't going back there again. And now, having totally disowned Nicky, I felt like Judas. I didn't understand why I was doing it. All I knew was that I didn't want to lose Maria – wise, loving and beautiful, she seemed pretty much perfect for me. Maria had a wonderful stillness about her that filled me with calm – I had never felt so at peace in my life. But that didn't last long. The next morning, as I emerged from Maria's hut, I was greeted by Bhagwan Singh. 'How is your wife?' he said jokily. 'Did you have a vigorous night?'

I couldn't see Mama Singh sharing the joke. It was time to leave.

Chapter 25

Golf on the Dunes

The night train to Jodhpur was quiet. Having agreed to meet
Maria again in Pushkar (she wanted a few more days in Khuri)
I was now sitting in an empty four-bunk compartment at
Jaiselmer station, 'Ooh, this is nice,' I thought happily. 'A
whole compartment to myself? That's unheard of in India. I'm
going to do a special chant to celebrate!'

But just as I retrieved my book and beads, and the train began to leave the station, I heard a sudden clattering of footsteps
outside on the platform. And out of all the empty carriages on
that train, a very smart, very sweaty Indian businessman chose
mine to jump into.

He looked at me and I looked at him. And then I chose to
ignore him and put my hands together and started chanting.
Well, he seemed to find that fascinating. Instead of respectfully
sitting to one side, he sat on the bunk bang opposite and stared
at me with two burning, coal- black eyes.

It was the weirdest experience of my life. 'Nam myoho
renge kyo, Nam myoho renge kyo,' I intoned sonorously, but I
wasn't feeling celebratory anymore. Because instead of the
nice heart-shaped spot on the wall I had chosen to chant to, I
now found myself concentrating on the bright red *tikka* dot

between this guy's eyebrows.

A mood of stubbornness overcame me. 'How rude!' I thought angrily. 'Well, I'm not having it. I'm going to chant all night long if necessary.'

Fortunately, it wasn't necessary very long. Half an hour later, at the next station, my strange companion jumped up as suddenly as he had arrived, and made to leave the train.

Just before he did so, however, he paused and looked back.

'Excuse me, sir,' he said. 'Have you heard about Jesus?'

*

My reasons for being back in Jodhpur were twofold. Firstly, my old friend Col Fateh Singh had arranged an interview with the Maharajah there. This was an opportunity not to be missed. Secondly, I had got wind of a cache of valuable Maria Theresa Austro-Hungarian *thaler* coins going cheap in the night market. I wasn't going to miss those either.

The Maharajah, when I was introduced to him, did not stand on ceremony. 'Ah, Mr Frank Kusy. You are the English travel writer, yes?' He was wearing a wide red and white polka-dotted kurta top and a big, moustachioed grin.

I didn't know quite how to respond. Should I bow? Should I genuflect? Should I offer to kiss his ring? Fateh hadn't briefed me at all.

'Pleased to meet you...your Majesty,' I said lamely, stooping a bit to show a degree of reverence.

'Call me "Bubbles",' said the portly young royal, laughingly offering me his hand. 'All my friends do.'

We were sitting in his small private study at the back of the stately Umaid Bhawan Palace, which now doubled up as a hotel. A very serious-looking servant had just brought in 'real English' tea and Bubbles and Fateh were nibbling enthusiastically on Scottish shortbread biscuits from a solid silver plate.

'You must stay with us tonight,' said Bubbles. 'But first…we will play some golf.'

I nearly choked on my cup of Earl Grey. Golf? Was he having a laugh? All that was on view out of the latticed stone window were sand dunes, for as far as the eye could see.

The Maharajah giggled at my bafflement, then crossed the room to a metal filing cabinet. Opening the top drawer, he pulled out a square piece of wood, which was covered one side with what appeared to be artificial grass.

'We will of course, very naturally, be needing this,' he announced. 'This will be our "turf".'

'We will of course also be needing *this*,' added Fateh,

whipping out a bottle of Johnnie Walker from his jacket pocket.

My eyes widened. Here I was with two of the most influential men in Rajasthan, and I was about to play golf in the desert on Blue Label whisky.

'Err...how many holes will we be playing?' I enquired nervously.

'Do not worry, my good chap,' said Bubbles, his eyes twinkling with mischief. 'It is not the full round...eight holes will do!'

Well, we didn't get to eight holes. We barely managed two. Bubbles placed his piece of 'turf' on the ground, teed off a perfect shot to the first hole...and the ball never hit the sand. Instead, there was a yelp of surprise and a figure popped up from behind one of the dunes, rubbing a sore head.

'What is that fellow doing there?' said Bubbles, rather crossly. 'He is ruining my game completely!'

It took the distressed Maharajah six more shots to get his ball in the first hole (Fateh and I had discreetly agreed to let him have the advantage) and sixteen to down the second. The reason it took that many was that the bottle of Johnnie Walker was now quite empty, and Fateh had produced another one.

'I am thinking I am hearing the gong for supper,' slurred Bubbles as the prospect of a third hole defeated him. 'Shall we call it a day?'

That was not the end of my royal experience. The next morning, still half-sozzled from my massive intake of alcohol, I was woken in my luxury palace suite by a knock at the door at 8am. 'Who the hell is this?' I thought blearily. 'I'm going to cripple his bell finger!'

Nothing prepared me for what came next. I wrapped a skimpy little towel around my waist, and strode to the door and opened it. And there stood two neat rows of turbaned and cummerbunded soldiers, their sabres held high and glinting in the sun, all grinning at me expectantly. Then two of them dashed out and rolled out the red carpet. 'Now that's what I call service!' I thought to myself. 'What are they going to do for an encore?'

The answer was 'nothing'. They quickly realised their mistake, nodded in apology, and shifted the carpet six feet to the left.

Rajiv Gandhi was staying next door.

Chapter 26

Aliens in India

Having obtained my precious Maria Theresa coins in Jodhpur market (Fateh brokered the deal and got me a really good price) I bade my jovial friend farewell and travelled onto Pushkar. 'I can't wait to see Maria again,' I thought as I boarded the two rupee pilgrim bus over the Snake Mountain from Ajmer. 'Only half an hour to go!'

But the bus didn't take half an hour. It took twice that long because of the blind cow. The cow wandered onto the bus at Ajmer and – with no-one allowed to stop it – sat down at the back. All the pilgrims shuffled dutifully to one side and made way for it. Then, somewhere near the top of the mountain, it clambered clumsily to its feet and tried to get off again. The bus ground to a halt, the cow was gently persuaded back in, and the passengers took it in turns to pat it for good luck. In Pushkar at last, the sacred animal dismounted, looked around sightlessly for a bit, and then got back on the bus.

I was glad to be back in Pushkar. It was a magical place, my second 'home' in the world, and I knew I would be returning time and again. I well remembered my first impressions of the place: a small jewel in the navel of India, ablaze with its colourful mix of pilgrims, hippies, merchants, and holy men, its outdoor menagerie of cows, pigs, dogs, and monkeys. The ancient buildings were all whitewashed and flaky, the lake full of leaping carp and small turtles (holy to Brahma), and the winding, sleepy marketplace dotted with browsing backpackers.

The first thing I did on arrival was to see whether Maria had checked in yet. 'Yes, madam come today,' said the receptionist at the Pushkar Palace hotel. 'She is presently in garden.'

She was indeed in the garden, but she was not alone. An animated Rajasthani man on crutches was talking to her. 'Who is that angry-looking guy?' I wondered. 'Hmm…this looks like a private conversation. I'll leave them alone.'

Going up to my favourite room, no 111, I had a pleasant surprise. A huge heart-shaped ring of bright red rose petals adorned the bed, and a single bloom of fragrant frangipani sat on my pillow. 'Aw,' I thought. 'She loves me.'

How much she loved me became apparent a few minutes later, when Maria appeared. 'Don't say a thing,' she murmured huskily. 'Just come here and open your present.'

Two hours later, having opened my present quite a few times, I lit a cigarette. 'So you missed me, then?' I said with a grin. 'How was Khuri?'

'You were right to leave when you did,' she grinned back. 'Bhagwan saw the funny side of us getting together, but when Mama found out about it, she threw a blue fit. I had to leave the day after you – she doesn't approve of sex before marriage!'

As I gazed once more into those big, blue eyes of hers, wondering yet again where all this was going, I also found myself thinking – for some reason – of the strange Indian she had been chatting to in the garden.

'He's not your ordinary Indian,' Maria said when I brought the subject up. 'He's different. You should go talk to him.'

So, an hour or so later, having showered and taken some food, I sought out this guy. His name was Ram Narayan, and he certainly was different. 'I do not want money,' he said proudly. 'I just want chance.'

I regarded the hunched, fierce-looking figure before me. Maria had confided that he'd had a bad injection from a doctor when he was a child, and he had contracted polio which had withered both his legs. What chance could I give him?

'Erm…well, what can you do?' I cautiously enquired.

'I can ride camel!' said Ram, adjusting the bright turban on his head and twirling his long moustachios.

That gave me an idea. Khuri had been great for camel-trekking, but Pushkar – which was far nearer to Delhi and more accessible to foreign tourists – could be even better. The dunes started the minute one walked out of town, and the desert-scapes were more diverse and interesting.

And so 'Ram's Desert Experience', Pushkar's very first camel-trek company was born. The deal was simple. I bought Ram three camels (total cost $100). In return Ram agreed to take me and my friends for free treks into the desert whenever we hit town. It was the only way he would accept my 'charity.'

'You've done a good deed there,' said Maria, giving me a big hug. But I was not so sure. By some karmic quirk, good deeds – like taking on Bernard as a partner, for example – had a habit of coming back and biting me in the bum.

I hoped this one would be different.

*

In between buying Ram his camels, I took Maria for a tour up the single long market street which tracked round the northern end of the holy lake.

'What do you think of Pushkar, then?' I asked her. 'Is it as good as you expected?'

'Well, it's like a mini Jaiselmer with a holy lake, isn't it?' she smiled in reply. 'All these mediaeval alleys, quaint old houses, sleepy backstreet temples and shady banyan trees parked with dozy dogs, camels and cows. But then you've got the backdrop of stark desert and two towering hilltop temples which make you feel you're in a quasi-Mediterranean resort. I *love* it!'

At the bottom of the market, I bought five beautiful mirror embroidered jackets from a barrel-bellied old rogue called Narendas. I would have bought more, but a brief inspection of the rest of his stock revealed that none of the other jackets had pockets. They also appeared to have no collars and no sleeves. 'Sewing machine not working...broken,' was Narendas's excuse, but then, just to tease us, he fished out one coat with sleeves, pockets *and* a collar. 'This one has embroidery on backside', he announced. '*Backside* is expensive!' Narendas was pleased with his little joke and allowed himself a protracted cackling wheeze. A crimson cavern of teeth blossomed forth as he laughed and a red gob of *paan* juice was jettisoned into the street. He reminded Maria of a fat pirate, a very fat pirate. 'How can Narendas be so big,' she whispered, 'when he doesn't eat meat?' The answer was simple. Narendas *did* eat meat. He also drank whisky, more than a quart a day. Which probably explained why his coats had no pockets.

Further up the narrow, cobbled market street, we came across a silver guy called Lalit Kumar. Lalit wore a practised look of mourning on his face, and Maria thought he must come from a long line of undertakers. Every time we asked Lalit a price on anything, he looked perplexed, then morose, then downright funereal. He shuffled to the back of his shop, meditated a bit, came back again and said 'I geeeeve yoouu...'— followed by a price. If we questioned the price, his face screwed up like a prune and he whined 'Why you make like theeese?' And every time we tried to leave his shop, he gave us an injured look and produced something new to buy. I felt quite sorry for Lalit, until I realised this tragic act was all part of his sales ploy.

'I think he's a con artist,' commented Maria as we came away from Lalit's with three times more silver than I could actually afford. 'No, he's just an artist,' I laughed. 'I can learn a lot from him!'

After lunch, to my great surprise, I chanced across my old friend Dave from Thailand in a tailor's shop.

'What are you doing here?' I said with a chuckle. 'I thought you'd gone back to Vancouver!'

The ruddy-faced young Canadian grinned. 'Yeah, well, I got on the plane and saw all the miserable faces staring back at me, and got off again. I rebooked to India and have been hanging out in Pushkar ever since!'

Maria stared at Dave in disbelief. He was wearing a pair of tie-dye underpants on his head.

'Oh, don't mind me,' he said, catching her look. 'Frank will tell you. I'm a crazy guy.'

'So what *are* you doing here?' I repeated the question.

Dave tipped me a wink. 'I'm here buying clothing for a friend.'

'Really?' I exclaimed, my eyebrows going and staying on hoist. 'I never had you down as a businessman!'

'Man, oh man, it's so easy. I just choose stuff and bundle it up and send it from the post office, and this dude I know back home with a market stall pays me a hundred bucks a week.'

'Is it really that easy?'

'Oh yeah,' said Dave, casually removing his trademark flip flop and whapping a fly. 'Though I have noticed one thing.'

'What's that?'

'Well, it's kinda freaky, but as far as most Pushkar people are concerned, you are an alien. In fact, all of us Westerners are aliens. We come from a place that none of them have been to, or are ever likely to go to, and we wander round with an apparently endless supply of rupees to spend. Not only that, but we dress in weirdo hippy clothes, we eat (to them) tasteless crap like pancakes, chips and falafels, and we have completely different bodies, because we prefer to sit in chairs instead of on the ground. We also like to spend time with our own—we huddle together in crowded little cafes or restaurants, and rumour has it that we actually cohabit with each other outside the bounds of matrimony.'

Maria and I exchanged a secret smirk. We were remembering Khuri.

'The most successful Indians,' continued Dave, 'are the ones who have learnt to communicate properly with aliens. They know a few words of our language, they have the ability to make strange-looking alien clothing, and they have worked out (even though they totally disagree with) what we like and what we don't like. That's why all the rooftop restaurants here with "western-style buffets" do so well, and why tailors travel halfway round India to get people like me Varanasi prayer-shawls which are normally worn by the relatives of dead Hindus. They know you come from a different planet, man, but they just don't care as long as you give them lots of rupees.'

'That's a bit cynical, isn't it?' I queried.

'Not really,' countered Dave. 'I mean, take a guy like my tailor here. He's got his standard 20 words of English, ranging from 'Yes, please,' to 'Order coming, baba,' and that's all he needs to make pots of money. Any other Indians who try to intervene while he's doing a deal are shushed into silence because it is *his* job to deal with aliens. And he never says anything bad, because aliens are sensitive to being let down. Instead, he just acts out a part, in practised broken English, so that he makes more, not less, money. I mean, you go up to him and say "Why are these silk saree dresses 50 rupees when they were only 40 rupees last week?" and he'll mumble apologetically "Dresses expensive, please. All other buyer pay, now *you* pay – okay, baba?" And you know you've got no choice because everybody else has made a mint out of his stuff and have come back, like you, to quadruple their order with him. He's got you over a barrel, but he won't actually say so, because if he makes you lose face you might fly back to your planet and never come back!'

'Great theory, Dave,' I said, scratching my head. 'Though we aren't the first Westerners to touch down on Planet India. The first batch of us aliens arrived during the Raj. That's where standards of speech and dress were first set. Then, 30 years later, the second wave arrived but they were all hippies and freaks heading here for the weed and the beaches. And they spoke foul language and dressed down in saris and local dress, which really confused the Indians. So now *they're* the ones dressed in suits and speaking the best Queen's English, and they only tolerate us because they're waiting for us to transmogrify back into the *first* batch of aliens!'

'Fascinating, ain't it?' concluded Dave. 'And nowhere more true than right here in Pushkar. Just have a look around, man. Aliens have carte blanche to break every commandment in the Pushkar guidebook. They can smoke ganga, they can drink alcohol (okay, only after dark or in their rooms), they can kiss and hold hands in public, and they can take photographs of the holy lake. All these things are forbidden by Hindu law, but aliens have lots of dollars so they can do what they like and all the locals turn a blind eye. That's why Pushkar is so cool – it's not like India at all!'

*

To celebrate our reunion, Dave took us for some food at what he called the 'Techno Café'—the small cafe opposite the post office, where all the donkeys hung out and where *bhang* (marijuana) lassis went for ten rupees a throw. And hardly had we sat down, than a wedding procession came up the road. It was a typical Rajasthani wedding procession, with the groom up on a horse, lots of colourful ladies dancing around him with pots on their heads, and in the forefront was a band, which took up the whole square. And the band was heading towards the Techno Cafe, which happened to be on a hairpin bend. So we got up for a better look and what did we see? *Another* band coming the other way! I fished out my camera, thinking to myself 'This is going to be good!' And indeed it was, because as the two incredibly loud and incredibly discordant bands rounded the corner, there was a head-on collision, and the whole mass of people involved just ground to a halt for about 15 minutes. Then they kind of worked it out and merged and flowed through each other, with both these bands working overtime trying to be heard over the other one.

Maria liked Dave. He reminded her of her younger brother, who was a stand-up comedian in Sydney. She was particularly entertained when Dave and I began regaling each other with all the amusing hotel and traffic signs we'd seen around India:

Hotel Jai—Be our Cosy Guest tonight, wake up Gay in the morning (Kodaikanal)

International Frunk Phone Service—Dial and Talk Foreign at Once (Jaiselmer)

Hotel Traffic Jam—Veg and non-Veg (Delhi)

Keep a Strict Watch around Yourself! (Darjeeling)

Mocking of Ladies is Punishable (Pushkar)

Five minutes for Tea and Urine (unidentified bus stop)

Hop along in life, or cross the road carefully (Delhi)

Dear Mr Motorist, if you drive like Hell, you will see it soon (Jaipur)

Let Pa drive, Ma sit behind (Madras)

When you approach a corner, get Horny (Simla)

Don't gossip—let Him drive (Mount Abu)

Darling, do not Nag while I am Driving (Manali)

The last few, I told Maria, were the creation of Public Works Department 'poets', who were notoriously sexist. They were also responsible for other warning signs like 'Family Awaits—Please Oblige' (a direct appeal to the paternal instinct in every Indian driver) and 'Beware of Distracting View!'— which had nearly taken my bus off a cliff at Kodaikanal. My driver had been more distracted by the *sign* than the view.

The following day, leaving Dave to have his nipple pierced in the market, Maria and I prepared to leave Pushkar. As I packed away my stuff, I discovered a tribe of large cockroaches in my sink. They were feeding on – of all things – the residue of last night's Oraldene mouthwash. I rang for room service and a bearded ruffian appeared with a large broom and battered them all to death on the bathroom floor. 'That was a bit drastic,' said Maria, rather horrified. 'This is India,' I told her. 'India invented drastic.'

Both of us were quiet on the night bus to Delhi. Our whirlwind romance was coming to an end, and we knew it. From time to time, Maria looked at me sadly and I gave her a sad look back. We held hands, and imagined an alternate universe where we didn't live thousands of miles apart, and where we could continue our India dream forever.

Six hours later, as we neared Delhi airport, I made a rash promise. 'Look,' I said. 'Whatever happens, no matter what, let's meet up here again next year – same time, same place. I'm not going to lose you.' And was rewarded by a nod and a shy smile which drove away the sadness. I had no idea how I was going to fulfil this promise. All that I knew was that I had something precious here. It wasn't all just an illusion, was it?

At the airport, having torn myself from Maria's tearful embrace, I faced another difficult hurdle—how to smuggle 28 kilos of silver and handicrafts onto my plane as 'hand luggage'. There was no way I was going to check it into the main hold. I had heard too many stories of dishonest baggage handlers to risk that. So I shoved it into the X-ray machine at security check and waited for it to come out the other end. But it didn't. It had become stuck there. Two burly policemen turned up to yank it out, and when they did so, loose bags of silver jewellery flew all over the place. 'You need all this *silver* for the plane?' hissed one of the policemen and fixed me with a predatory grin. I nodded helplessly and waited—anticipating a huge fine or confiscation of our goods—while he went off to consult with his colleague. Finally, he returned and did something quite unexpected. Bending low, with a furtive look on his face, he whispered 'Give me MONEE!'

Unable to believe my luck, I emptied out my pockets and came up with 47 rupees in small change. It was only £1.50 but he seemed quite happy with that. So happy indeed, that he shook my hand and waved me onto the plane.

Chapter 27

Birth of a Market Trader

The business had a rocky start. For one thing, Bernard had bought a lot of the wrong stuff – the marble chess sets from Agra which had chips in them and which nobody wanted, the silver-plated tea services which were already turning suspiciously rusty, and the so-called 'gold' jewellery which had gone a strange green.

I also had a few turkeys from my side. My valuable antique Victorian rupees had been rendered non-valuable by some Indian cowboy 'cleaning' them in silver dip, my precious Maria Theresa *thaler* coins had been declared 'fake' when I had them valued at Sotheby's, and half the stones had fallen out of Lalit Kumar's 'first class' jewellery. As for the hero who mucked up my 1000 banyan leaf Christmas cards by writing 'Happy Critmas!' inside them, well, he was definitely off my Critmas card list.

The day was saved by the high grade gemstones Fateh helped me choose in Jaipur's seedy Johari Bazar. 'Buy my packet! Buy my packet!' the throng of grimy workers had cried as they clambered over each other to sell me stones they'd smuggled out – down their dhotis or under their armpits – during their lunch breaks. I had no idea what I was doing: all that

I knew was that I was having the time of my life. 'What a buzz!' I'd shouted to the Colonel. '"Spiritual experience" or not, I was born to do this!" And although I hadn't managed to sell the stones back home in Hatton Garden – they weren't quite high grade enough – I did manage to move them up in the Jewish Quarter of Sheffield, and made a very handsome profit.

My other saviour was my mother. She totally disapproved of my new vocation – 'Do you want to be a barrow boy all your life? – but she it was who helped set up my first stall in London's Martin in the Fields market. She shoved the chess sets and tea services to one side – 'What's this tat? They won't sell! – and promoted the silver jewellery and 'one offs' like the beautiful Moghul paintings I'd bought in Udaipur, the equally beautiful batik paintings I'd bought in Solo, and the fantastic picture of a roaring lion which had been painted by a blind artist in Chiang Mai. By the end of my first day, the stall was nearly empty and I returned home to Nicky in high spirits.

'Look!' I glowed in exultation. 'Over a thousand pounds!' And as I threw the banknotes in the air and they floated slowly downwards, we both tore our clothes off and made love – for the first time in months – on the crinkly, wrinkly carpet of our new-found wealth.

Just before Christmas, as I stood in a shoebox full of snow counting yet more cash, Bernard turned up – miraculously re- covered from his terminal illness – and demanded half of my takings. 'Here,' I said, wheeling out the useless tea services and even more useless chess sets. 'That, plus your original stake of three grand, is all you'll get out of me. Now, sod off!'

Nicky and I had a lot of good things going for us, but the age difference wasn't one of them. She could have passed for a schoolgirl, and I looked old enough to be her dad. Indeed, when it had come round to Father's Day, the waiter who served us food at an expensive restaurant in Soho looked at us both and said, 'Here's a menu for you, young lady. Now, where would your father like to sit?' And Nicky's mother, who was ultra-protective of her after finding out what her real dad had been up to, was fond of referring to me as 'the old Jew'. 'Who's that old Jew getting out of the car?' she'd asked Nicky when I first came round the house. 'Look at him. Black hat, black coat, black beard, and thick, round spectacles. I bet heI bet he's on the way to the synagogue!' On the plus side, we had Buddhism. We had after all met at a Buddhist meeting – where everyone but Nicky had laughed at me over the Polish biker chick – and we had this strong, rather naïve, belief that a couple who chanted together stayed together. I still remembered, for instance, the night in Bali – three days after our 'wedding' – when Nicky had talked me out of a jealous mood (she had gone off somewhere without telling me) by making me chant 'in harmony' with her. 'I know what you're doing,' she'd scolded me. 'You're deliberately chanting out of tune. Come on, pull yourself together, you're better than this. Try and tune in with me!' And tune in I did, and half an hour later, we were making mad, passionate love again.

But love, lust and Buddhism was never going to be enough.

As I was about to find out...

Chapter 28

The Final Curtain

'Who's Maria?' said Nicky, shoving the letter in my face. 'What have you been up to, you sneaky, two-faced bastard?

Maria? What was Maria doing writing me a letter? And what did it say? It had to be bad – there was no mistaking the flash of ice in Nicky's cold, green eyes.

'Err…I don't know what you're talking about. And what are you doing, opening up my letters?'

'Good thing I did, mister. I was expecting something important in the mail this morning, so I opened up *all* the letters. You've got some explaining to do!'

'Like what?' My mind was racing.

'Like having an affair with another woman in India, for one. I knew I should have gone out there with you!'

'I squirmed. 'Err…well, yes, maybe you should have. Look, see things from my side – we've been like strangers for months, with you staying out practically every night. And the only time you wrote while I was in India was all about Bernard and the business. I was both angry and lonely. Things just…happened.'

'Like shagging her and telling her we were over?'

'I did *not* tell her we were over!' I replied hotly. 'I just said…erm…that we were having problems.'

'Well, we've certainly got a problem now,' huffed Nicky, her pretty, doll-like features twisted into a grotesque leer. 'She's been trying to track you down for weeks – she wants to come see you here in the U.K.!'

'Oh God, no.'

'Oh God, yes. Ironic, isn't it? All this time, you've been giving me hell – no, not in words, I know you've been buttoning your lip – but in cold, distant looks and holding back from making love to me – when you've done the very same thing. You said I was staying out all those nights, do you think I enjoyed that? Anything was better than sitting at home while you wrote your bloody books, eating all my meals alone. I know the real reason you found someone else – you'd fallen out of love with me, and didn't even know it!'

'Well,' I snapped rather brutally. 'It was getting very difficult to love someone who didn't love themselves. You've been punishing yourself ever since you told me about Simon, haven't you? Didn't you realise you were punishing me too?'

We looked at each other, I mean *really* looked at each other, for the very first time.

'It's not going to work, is it?' said Nicky at last. 'I thought I had trust issues, that I could never make a commitment to a man, but you take the biscuit. Okay, so I let the side down with Simon, I'll have to live with that for the rest of my life. But come on, actually falling in love with someone else – because that's what happened, isn't it? – is the cruellest kind of payback. When were you going to tell me about all this? Never?'

I had no answer, and all of a sudden – through a few scrawled lines on a piece of paper from the other side of the world – it was over. The very next day, despite my protestations for her to stay, Nicky silently packed her bags and moved out of my life forever.

Postscript

Christmas Day found me back at my mum's, counting all the money I had taken from the market stall. It was a jaw-staggering amount– over ten thousand pounds. 'Well, this *is* ironic,' I thought to myself. 'Now I have lots of money for a big wedding…but nobody to get married to!' Nicky was out of the question now, and unfortunately, Maria also. I had read Maria's letter over and over, and with increasing anger and frustration. What was she doing, writing to me at Nicky's and breaking her promise not to interfere in our relationship? Not to mention inviting herself to the U.K. unbidden? Why on earth hadn't she phoned me? I had left her my mum's number – she could easily have got in touch with me there. But no, now that I thought about it, I had scribbled that number on an old fag packet as we'd hurriedly parted ways at Delhi airport. I could easily have missed a digit or two.

Whatever, if I had learned anything from this year by now, it was that 'GURs' (geographically undesirable relationships) were not a good thing for me – I wouldn't have been happy living in Australia, and Maria, with her music career just taking off there, would never have put down roots in England. I had to be realistic (for once) – Maria and I just didn't have a future.

As 1989 slid into 1990, another future opened up to me, however.

I was about to become a rupee millionaire…

185

~ *THE END* ~

A Note from the Author

To subscribe to my mailing list just paste **http://eepurl.com/bvhenb** into your web browser and follow the link. You'll be the first to know when my next book is ready to be launched!

Hi folks – Frank here!

Thank you so much for reading my book, I do hope you enjoyed it. If you did, I'd love it if you could leave a few words on Amazon as a review. Not only are reviews crucial in getting an author's work noticed, but I personally love reviews and I read them all!

I'd also love it if you checked out my other travel memoirs: *Too Young to be Old: From Clapham to Kathmandu* **http://smarturl.it/TooYoungToBeOld**, *Kevin and I in India* **http://smarturl.it/KevinIndia15**, and *Rupee Millionaires* **http://smarturl.it/RupeeM15**. Not to mention (though I just did!) my two quirky, award-winning cat books *Ginger the Gangster Cat* **http://smarturl.it/Gingergangster15** and Ginger the Buddha Cat **http://smarturl.it/Ginger15**. Thanks!

Oh, and if you like reading memoirs, there's a really cool Facebook group called 'We Love Memoirs'. We'd love it if you dropped in to chat to the author and lots of other authors and readers here:

https://www.facebook.com/groups/welovememoirs/

P.S. Here's where you can find me on Twitter:
https://twitter.com/Wussyboy

And where to catch me on Facebook:
https://www.facebook.com/frank.kusy.5?ref=tn_tnmn

And if you get the urge, you can always email me:
sparky-frank@hotmail.co.uk

Acknowledgements

Big thanks to Ida of Amygdaladesign (for my lovely cover), to my wonderful wife 'Madge' (for saying 'Yes, that's good,' or 'That's crap,' in all the right places), to Cherry Gregory (for the final beta read), to Nick Kenrick (for the pukka Pushkar pic), and to the amazing Roman Laskowski for yet another round of meticulous editing and formatting. Top job, mate!

Oh, and a special mention to my good friend Philip Moseley, for inspiring me to write this book. I don't dare meet with Philip again in the near future – every time he says 'Jump', I find myself saying 'How high?'

Frank Kusy

About the author

FRANK KUSY is a professional travel writer with nearly thirty years experience in the field. He has written guides to India, Thailand, Burma, Malaysia, Singapore and Indonesia. Of his first work, the travelogue *Kevin and I in India* (1986), the Mail on Sunday wrote: 'This book rings so true of India that most of us will be glad we don't have to go there ourselves.'

Born in England (of Polish-Hungarian parents), Frank left Cardiff University for a career in journalism and worked for a while at the Financial Times. India is his first love, the only country he knows which improves on repeated viewings. He still visits for business and for pleasure at least once a year. He lives in Surrey, England, with his wife Andrea and his little cat Sparky.

GRINNING BANDIT BOOKS

A word from our sponsors…

If you enjoyed *Off the Beaten Track*, please check out these other brilliant books:

Too Young to be Old: From Clapham to Kathmandu, Kevin and I in India, Dial and Talk Foreign at Once, Rupee Million-aires, The Reckless Years, Ginger the Gangster Cat, Ginger the Buddha Cat – all by Frank Kusy (Grinning Bandit Books).

Weekend in Weighton and *Warwick the Wanderer* – both by Terry Murphy (Grinning Bandit Books).

The Ultimate Inferior Beings by Mark Roman (Cogwheel Press).

Scrapyard Blues and *The Albion* – both by Derryl Flynn (Grinning Bandit Books).

The Girl from Ithaca, The Walls of Troy, and *Percy the High Flying Pig* – all by Cherry Gregory (Grinning Bandit Books).

Flashman and the Sea Wolf, Flashman and the Cobra, Flashman in the Peninsula, and *Flashman's Escape* – all by Robert Brightwell (Grinning Bandit Books).

…and a special mention for a non-Grinning Bandit book:
The Worst Man on Mars – by Mark Roman and Corben Duke

Made in the USA
Las Vegas, NV
04 June 2022

49789498R00115